W9-AVM-220

A HISTORICAL READER

Founding a NATION

nextext

Printed in the United States of America

ISBN 0-618-00366-5

8 — QVK — 06 05 04

Table of Contents

Throughout the reader, vocabulary words appear in boldface type and are footnoted. Specialized or technical words and phrases appear in lightface type and are footnoted.

Stirrings
of Rebellion

Jefferson's World

BY JOHN DOS PASSOS

In his book The Head and Heart of Thomas Jefferson, *John Dos Passos examines what everyday life was like in the British colonies when the rebellion that became the Revolutionary War was first stirring. Thomas Jefferson was the author of the Declaration of Independence, a Virginia legislator for 40 years, and the third President of the United States. His love of politics and the law began when he was a student at the College of William and Mary in Williamsburg, the capital of the Virginia Colony. The first excerpt describes his trip to college and the city he finds there. The events in the second excerpt occur after the colonies' boycott of British goods has forced the British government to back down from the Stamp Act. Here Jefferson describes a colonial legislature—this one in Maryland.*

[1760] When Jefferson rode into Williamsburg splashing through the muddy ruts in the raw weather of the **retarded**[1] spring of 1760, his seventeenth birthday was only a few days ahead. All the long ride down the valley of the James, through shaggy woodlands

---

[1] **retarded**—delayed.

alternating with the cultivated lands where the planters worked their uncomprehending slaves so hard hacking the wilderness into some semblance of the neat English countryside, his blood must have tingled with anticipation of city life; and the library full of books, and Hunter's printshop with new publications from England and gazettes fresh from the press with their dispatches announcing new victories for Mr. Pitt;[2] and candlelit ballrooms rustling with pretty girls, and pleasant friends to gossip with round the punchbowl; and blooded[3] horses to match on the racetrack. . . .

Jefferson was arriving on the edge of one of the "public times" when the place was full of bustle and must have seemed to the colonists a tiny fragment of metropolitan London. The burgesses[4] met during the early part of March and the session of the General Court was coming in April. Some of the members of the governor's Council may well have already been lumbering about the rutted streets in their coaches. Preening their fine feathers for the official call on the governor, families recently arrived from upcountry might be seen at the doors of their friends' houses, men in silver lace and cocked hats, and ladies in satins and silks, and servants in livery holding the heads of sleek horses champing in the polished harness of berlins or chariots. The Raleigh and the other inns and lodginghouses swarmed with lawyers in sadcolored traveling clothes and delegates coming and going, their brows heavy with public business. In the common rooms, amid the smoke of clay pipes; the tables resounded with the banging of diceboxes. The merchants in the scattered stores round the Exchange had set out the latest goods arrived from England. Cattle and pigs and slaves were in pens ready to be auctioned off in the open

---

[2] Mr. Pitt—William Pitt, the British politician who supported the American colonists against the harsh policies of the Tories in Parliament.

[3] blooded—thoroughbred.

[4] burgesses—elected members of the House of Burgesses, a branch of the colonial Virginia legislature.

space between. In his shop the wigmaker and his apprentices were busy combing and curling gentlemen's wigs for official functions. . . .

* * *

[1766] After various **misadventures**[5] . . . Jefferson drove into Annapolis. There he found the Marylanders busy celebrating the Stamp Act's[6] repeal, which had been accomplished, so everybody believed, through the good offices of the colonists' friend, William Pitt. There were bonfires and illuminations and drunken crowds round the taverns that night.

Next morning Jefferson admired the snug little harbor, the lovely views of Chesapeake Bay and the new brick mansions of some of the wealthy planters. As much as architecture, the process of government was becoming the central passion of his life; so, naturally, since the Maryland Assembly happened to be sitting, he lost no time in sticking his nose in to see how their proceedings compared with those of the burgesses at Williamsburg. He was twenty-three, out of his home province for the first time; it is not surprising that he found little to admire: "Their upper & lower house, as they call them, sit in different houses. I went into the lower, sitting in an old courthouse, which judging from its form and appearance, was built in the year one. I was surprised on approaching it to hear as great a noise & hubbub as you will usually observe at a public meeting of the planters in Virginia. The first object which struck me after my entrance was the figure of a little man dressed but indifferently with a yellow queue wig on, and mounted in the judge's chair. This the gentleman who walked with me informed me was the speaker, a man of very **fair**[7] character, who by the bye,

---

[5] **misadventures**—mishaps.

[6] The Stamp Act was the first direct tax imposed by Britain on the American colonies.

[7] **fair**—marked by honesty and impartiality.

has very little the air of a speaker. At one end of the justice's bench stood a man whom in another place I should from his dress & phis[8] have taken for Goodall the lawyer in Williamsburg, reading a bill then before the house with a schoolboy tone & an abrupt pause at every half dozen words. This I found to be the clerk of the assembly. The mob (for such was their appearance) sat covered on the justice's and lawyers' benches, and were divided into little clubs amusing themselves in the common chit chat way. I was surprised to see them address the speaker without rising from their seats, and three four and five at a time without being checked. When a motion was made, the speaker instead of putting the question in the usual form only asked the gentlemen whether they chose that such a thing should be done, & was answered by a yes sir, or no sir: and tho' the voices appeared frequently to be divided, they never would go to the trouble of dividing the house,[9] but the clerk entered the resolutions, I supposed, as he thought proper. In short everything seems to be carried without the house in general's knowing what was proposed."

---

[8] dress & phis—short for "dress and physique"; appearance.

[9] dividing the house—actually counting the votes. Jefferson means that the clerk recorded the vote based on his own interpretation of a voice vote, without taking a count.

QUESTIONS TO CONSIDER

1. Why was Thomas Jefferson so excited on his ride into Williamsburg?

2. What was Jefferson's opinion of the Maryland Assembly? Give examples to support your view.

3. What British influences do you see in these descriptions of colonial America?

Ideas of the Enlightenment

Eighteenth-century political ideas were influenced by a movement known as the Enlightenment. Beginning in the mid-1600s, English philosophers Thomas Hobbes and John Locke explained where a government's authority came from and what rights were "natural."

In 1689, Parliament issued the "Declaration of Rights," asserting Enlightenment ideas for their government. In the Declaration, Parliament goes on record with their beliefs about the rights of those who are governed. Other philosophers expanded on these ideas about the nature of people and their relations with each other through government. Some argued that by joining together in a social contract, people became more moral. Jefferson and his contemporaries read the philosophers' thoughts and added their own. Together, these ideas helped form the world's understanding of what a government of free people should, and should not, be.

from *Leviathan*
by Thomas Hobbes[1]

The only way [for men] to erect . . . a Common Power [that] may be able to defend them from the invasion of [foreigners] and the injuries of one another, and thereby to secure them in such sort as that by their own industry and by the fruits of the Earth they may nourish themselves and live contentedly, is to confer all their power and strength upon one Man, or upon one Assembly of men, that may reduce all their Wills, by plurality of voices, unto one Will . . . and therein to submit their Wills, every one to his Will, and their Judgments to his Judgment. This is more than Consent or Concord, it is a real Unity of them all, in one and the same Person, made by Covenant of every man with every man, in such manner as if every man should say to every man, *I Authorize and give up my Right of Governing myself to this Man, or to this Assembly of men, on this condition, that thou give up thy Right to him, and Authorize all his Actions in like manner. . .*

from *Second Treatise on Government*
by John Locke[2]

The reason why men enter into society is the preservation of their property; and the end why they choose and authorize a legislative[3] is that there may be laws made and rules set, as guards and fences to the properties of all the members of the society, to limit the power and moderate the dominion of every part and member of the society. For since it can never be supposed to be the will of the society that the legislative should have a power to

---

[1] Published in 1651. Hobbes argued in favor of the absolute power of kings.

[2] Published in 1690. Locke argued that people have the right to dissolve a government that does not preserve the individual's right to life, liberty, and property.

[3] legislative—law-making body, such as Congress or Parliament.

destroy that which every one designs to secure . . ., whenever the legislators endeavor to take away and destroy the property of the people, or to reduce them to slavery under arbitrary power, they put themselves into a state of war with the people . . . .

. . . Such revolutions happen not upon every little mismanagement in public affairs. Great mistakes in the ruling part, many wrong and inconvenient laws, and all the slips of human frailty, will be born by the people without mutiny or murmur. But if a long rain of abuses, **prevarications**[4] and **artifices**,[5] all tending the same way, make the design visible to the people, and they cannot but feel what they lie under, and see whither they are going, [then] it is not to be wondered at that they should then rouse themselves and endeavor to put the rule into such hands which may secure to them the ends for which government was at first erected. . . .

The end of government is the good of mankind; and which is best for mankind, that the people should always be exposed to the boundless will of tyranny, or that the rulers should be sometimes liable to be opposed, when they grow exorbitant in the use of their power, and employ it for the destruction, and not the preservation of the properties of their people?

from *The English Declaration of Rights*

. . . And thereupon, the [members of both Houses of Parliament] pursuant to their respective letters and elections being now assembled in a full and free representative of this nation, taking into their most serious consideration the best means for attaining the ends aforesaid, do in the first place (as their ancestors

---

[4] **prevarications**—lies.

[5] **artifices**—tricks, ruses, ways of fooling people, double-dealings.

in like case have usually done) for the **vindicating**[6] and asserting their ancient rights and liberties, declare:

- That the pretended power of dispensing with laws or the execution of laws by regal authority as it hath been assumed and exercised of late is illegal.

- That the commission for erecting the late court of commissioners for ecclesiastical causes and all other commissions and courts of like nature are illegal and **pernicious**[7].

- That the levying money for or to the use of the crown by pretense of **prerogative**[8] without grant of parliament for a longer time or in other manner than the same is or shall be granted is illegal.

- That it is the right of the subjects to petition the king and all commitment and prosecutions for such petitioning are illegal.

- That the raising or keeping of a standing army within the kingdom in time of peace unless it be with consent of parliament is against law.

- That the subjects which are Protestants may have arms for their defense suitable to their conditions and as allowed by law.

- That election of members of parliament ought to be free.

- That the freedom of speech and debates or proceedings in parliament ought not to be impeached or questioned in any court or place out of parliament.

---

[6] **vindicating**—maintaining and defending.

[7] **pernicious**—destructive, malicious, harmful. This clause is a response to certain acts of James II that violated freedom of religion.

[8] **prerogative**—a hereditary or official right or privilege.

- That excessive bail ought not to be required nor excessive fines imposed nor cruel and unusual punishments inflicted.

- That jurors ought to be duly impaneled and returned and jurors which pass upon men in trials for high treason ought to be freeholders.[9]

- That all grants and promises of fines and forfeitures of particular persons before conviction are illegal and void.

- And that for redress of all grievances[10] and for the amending, strengthening and preserving of the laws parliaments ought to be held frequently.

And they do claim, demand and insist upon all and singular the premises as their undoubted rights and liberties and that no declarations, judgments, doings or proceedings to the prejudice of the people in any of the said premises ought in any wise to be drawn hereafter into consequence or example.

---

[9] freeholders—landowners.

[10] redress of all grievances—compensation for all injuries, correcting wrongs.

QUESTIONS TO CONSIDER

1. What does Hobbes say that people gain when they "erect a Common Power," that is, form a government? What do they give up?

2. How do Locke's arguments support the American colonists?

3. What parts of the English Declaration of Rights could support the colonists? Explain your answer.

Declaration of Rights and Grievances

BY THE STAMP ACT CONGRESS

In October 1765, the Stamp Act Congress, consisting of delegates from nine colonies, drew up a strongly worded protest against Britain's Stamp Act, which was scheduled to take effect the following month. To help cover the cost of maintaining troops in the colonies, Parliament planned to place a tax on all legal and commercial documents as well as on printed materials, such as newspapers and pamphlets. To prove the tax had been paid, all documents needed to carry a special stamp. In a bold and defiant act, the Stamp Act Congress issued the following Declaration of Rights and Grievances to the British government. Together with protests and boycotts in the colonies and the persuasion of the brilliant orator, William Pitt, in Parliament, the move succeeded. The Stamp Act was repealed.

October 19, 1765
Declaration of Rights

The members of this Congress, sincerely devoted, with the warmest sentiments of affection and duty to His Majesty's Person and Government, **inviolably**[1] attached to the present happy establishment of the Protestant succession, and with minds deeply impressed by a sense of the present and impending misfortunes of the British colonies on this continent; having considered as maturely as time will permit the circumstances of the said colonies, esteem it our indispensable duty to make the following declarations, of our humble opinions respecting the most essential rights and liberties of the colonists, and of the grievances under which they labor, by reason of several late Acts of Parliament.

I. That His Majesty's subjects in these colonies owe the same allegiance to the Crown of Great Britain, that is owing from his subjects born within the realm, and all due **subordination**[2] to that **august**[3] body, the Parliament of Great Britain.

II. That His Majesty's **liege**[4] subjects in these colonies, are entitled to all the inherent rights and privileges of his natural born subjects within the kingdom of Great Britain.

III. That it is inseparably essential to the freedom of a people, and the undoubted right of Englishmen, that no taxes be imposed on them, but with their own consent, given personally, or by their representatives.

---

[1] **inviolably**—securely.

[2] **subordination**—submission to authority.

[3] **august**—respected for reasons of age or high rank.

[4] **liege**—loyal.

IV. That the people of these colonies are not, and from their local circumstances cannot be, represented in the House of Commons in Great Britain.

V. That the only representatives of the people of these colonies are persons chosen therein by themselves, and that no taxes ever have been, or can be constitutionally imposed on them, but by their respective legislatures.

VI. That all supplies to the Crown being free gifts of the people, it is unreasonable and inconsistent with the principles and spirit of the British Constitution for the people of Great Britain to grant to His Majesty the property of the colonists.

VII. That trial by jury is the inherent and invaluable right of every British subject in these colonies.

VIII. That the late Act of Parliament entitled, "An Act for granting and applying certain Stamp Duties, and other Duties, in the British colonies and plantations in America, etc.," by imposing taxes on the inhabitants of these colonies, and the said Act, and several other Acts, by extending the jurisdiction of the Courts of **Admiralty**[5] beyond its ancient limits, have a **manifest**[6] tendency to **subvert**[7] the rights and liberties of the colonists.

IX. That the duties imposed by several late Acts of Parliament, from the peculiar circumstances of these colonies, will be extremely burthensome[8] and grievous; and from the scarcity of **specie**,[9] the payment of them absolutely impracticable.

---

[5] **Admiralty**—the department of the British government that once had control over all naval affairs.

[6] **manifest**—clear or obvious.

[7] **subvert**—destroy completely; ruin.

[8] burthensome—burdensome.

[9] **specie**—coined money.

X. That as the profits of the trade of these colonies ultimately center in Great Britain, to pay for the manufactures which they are obliged to take from thence, they eventually contribute very largely to all supplies granted there to the Crown.

XI. That the restrictions imposed by several late Acts of Parliament, on the trade of these colonies, will render them unable to purchase the manufactures of Great Britain.

XII. That the increase, prosperity, and happiness of these colonies, depend on the full and free enjoyment of their rights and liberties, and an **intercourse**[10] with Great Britain mutually affectionate and advantageous.

XIII. That it is the right of the British subjects in these colonies to petition the King or either House of Parliament.

Lastly, That it is the indispensable duty of these colonies to the best of sovereigns, to the mother country, and to themselves, to endeavor by a loyal and dutiful address to his Majesty, and humble applications to both Houses of Parliament, to procure the repeal of the Act for granting and applying certain stamp duties, of all clauses of any other Acts of Parliament whereby the jurisdiction of the Admiralty is extended as aforesaid, and of the other late Acts for the restriction of American commerce.

---

[10] **intercourse**—communication.

QUESTIONS TO CONSIDER

1. What was the Stamp Act Congress?

2. How would you describe the writing style of this document?

3. Which of the thirteen grievances do you think were most important to the colonists?

Boston Has a Tea Party

BY JOHN TEBBEL

Journalist John Tebbel is a revisionist historian. He wants to revise the picture earlier historians painted of "embattled farmers rising in defense of liberty, achieving independence by a series of heroic acts, led by an almost supernatural commander." In his book, Turning the World Upside Down, *Tebbel sets out to tell the story of the American Revolution as it was for the people who lived through it. His description of the Boston Tea Party shows the roles of merchants looking for profits, rebels eager to excite mobs, and a governor who has a private reason, as well as a public one, for enforcing the Tea Act.*

The Boston Tea Party is still celebrated as a patriotic reaction to an **onerous**[1] tax on tea that Americans refused to pay and, to make their point clear, threw a quantity of it into Boston Harbor. In reality, these duties had been in force for six years, and most of the time were either paid

---

[1] **onerous**—troublesome or oppressive.

without any trouble or simply disregarded. Nor was anyone forcing the colonists to buy the East India Company's tea.

The Tea Party, then, is no sudden explosion, and its origins may not even have been in Boston, but in Philadelphia, where for years certain merchants have been making handsome profits in smuggled tea and may have organized a quiet conspiracy in the major port cities to prevent any disturbance of their cozy arrangement.

If so, it seems at first they'll be successful. Before the Boston affair, when shipments of East India Company Tea arrive in Charleston, they're seized by customs officers and stacked away in damp cellars, where they will surely rot. This extraordinary behavior by such officials suggests that deals have been made. Other tea ships bound for the ports of Philadelphia and New York are given to understand they won't be permitted to land their cargoes and, taking the hint, return to England.

In Boston, however, already a **tinderbox,**[2] where the radicals are only waiting for an excuse, it's a different story, and there the unfortunate Hutchinson[3] is caught in a new crisis not of his making. He's opposed the tea duty since it was first imposed, and has frequently urged its repeal, but this exemplary resistance is overshadowed by the fact that he's secretly involved in tea merchandising himself, and in fact has invested much of his liquid capital in the East India Company. Worse, he owes his salary from the Crown (£1,500 yearly) to the income from the tea duty. Since no one has seriously objected to the tax, and because he believes the Philadelphia smugglers are trying to protect themselves

---

[2] **tinderbox**—potentially explosive place or situation.

[3] Hutchinson, Thomas—a fifth-generation New Englander appointed governor of the Massachusetts Colony by Britain.

from competition, he says the tea ships have every right to land.

The first of them, the *Dartmouth*, bearing 114 casks of tea, sails into Boston Harbor on November 28, 1773, and rides at anchor while the customs officers come aboard next day and the Boston activists demand that she return to England at once. But the *Dartmouth* is formally entered at customs and docks at Griffin's Wharf. When all its cargo, except for the tea, has been taken ashore, a military guard commanded by John Hancock throws a picket line around the ship to prevent any further unloading. In this 25-man guard is the young activist Paul Revere, armed with musket and bayonet.

This situation is shortly compounded by the arrival of two more tea ships, carrying a cargo of tea worth £18,000. Alarmed, "the Body," as the almost continuous mass meetings of citizens is now called, concludes that they'd better warn other ports along that part of the coast not to let in any tea ships. With five other express riders, who have been keeping the colonial Committees of Correspondence informed, Revere sets out on his first recorded ride of warning.

The town meetings, now taking place in Old South Church because Faneuil Hall is too small, are filled with thousands of non-legal voters, of whom Hutchinson has already complained. They mean to vote anyway. Sam Adams[4] brings in more recruits from neighboring towns, and they vote too. Schoolmasters even take their students to watch what is happily considered to be democracy in action, although many citizens, Whig and Tory alike, are shocked by what's going on, and fear the mob has taken over from duly constituted authority.

---

[4] Sam Adams—John Adams's younger brother, a rebel leader who this author describes as a rabble-rouser.

No one deplores this development more fervently than Hutchinson. To him, the immediate problem is clear. These ships can't leave the harbor legally until they're given customs clearance, and if they don't pay duty on their taxable goods within twenty days of arrival, their cargoes will be confiscated. That's the law. It will have to be enforced on December 17.

Once more Hutchinson stands on his principles and the law, hoping that the presence of British warships blocking the harbor will help him enforce it. Once more he's threatened by the mobs, in the streets and at the mass meetings. The radicals vilify him at every opportunity. At one meeting, Sam Adams roars with the authentic voice of **demagoguery,**[5] "Is he that shadow of a man scarce able to support his withered carcass on his **hoary**[6] head? Is he a representation of Majesty?"

Another **beleaguered**[7] man is the owner of the *Dartmouth,* a Captain Rotch. On the late afternoon of December 16, threatened with confiscation of his ship next day, he rides out to the governor's mansion in Milton to plead with Hutchinson to overlook the law for once, and let him leave the harbor with his tea *sans*[8] a customs clearance. Hutchinson refuses bluntly. He intends to enforce the law no matter what happens; the authority of Parliament, which he represents, is legitimate and must be upheld.

Thus the stage is set for the Tea Party, which has already been carefully planned, mostly in a tavern called the Green Dragon, which the radicals have virtually

---

[5] **demagoguery**—the methods or principles of a demagogue: a leader who obtains power by means of impassioned appeals to the emotions and prejudices of the populace.

[6] **hoary**—gray or white as if with age.

[7] **beleaguered**—harassed.

[8] *sans*—without.

taken over. Someone's even written a rallying song for the imminent Party:

> Rally, Mohawks! bring out your axes,
> And tell King George we'll pay no taxes
> On his foreign tea;
> His threats are vain, and vain to think
> To force our girls and wives to drink
> His vile Bohea!
> Then rally, boys, and hasten on
> To meet our chiefs at the Green Dragon!

What this **ditty**[9] lacks in substance, it makes up in inspiration. But the coming "Party" is one of the worst-kept secrets in a city that can scarcely have any. On that fateful December afternoon, while the *Dartmouth*'s owner is making his fruitless plea, crowds—perhaps as many as seven thousand—pass in ceaseless procession to and from the wharves for a look at the ships. All classes, high and low, are represented; many have come from surrounding towns. Having seen the ships, they roam the streets, peering in the windows of the Green Dragon, waiting for the climax of this drama.

At five forty-five on a gray, rainy afternoon, Captain Rotch appears at the packed town meeting in the Old South and reports his failure with the governor. "If called upon by the proper officers," he reports Hutchinson as saying, he would "attempt for his own security to land the tea." As though it's a prearranged signal—and no doubt it is—Sam Adams leaps to his feet and cries: "This meeting can do nothing more to save the country!" An answering roar erupts from the crowd, there are calls from the gallery, "To Griffin's Wharf," and "Boston Harbor's a teapot tonight!" The mob pours out of the building, followed by Hancock's **admonition,**[10]

---

[9] **ditty**—simple song.

[10] **admonition**—gentle reproof or warning.

"Let every man do what is right in his own eyes." What's right has already been determined in that substantial brick tavern on Union Street, the Green Dragon.

The planning has been a little ambiguous, however. On the one hand, it's been decided that young men not well known in Boston and therefore not easily recognized should do the work. On the other hand, some older conspirators fear looting and send along a few lieutenants to oversee the work, all of them familiar faces, while young Lendell Pitts, son of a rich merchant and well known to everyone, appears as commander-in-chief of the party and makes no effort at concealment.

There are other familiar faces among these barely disguised "Mohawks": Will Molineux;[11] Paul Revere, not disguised and taking a considerable risk since he's been married only two months; John Hancock; and of course, Sam Adams. The remainder of this war party of fake Indians, somewhere between 100 and 150 of them, are journeymen, apprentices, or strangers from other towns. Many of these, too, have failed to disguise themselves. The others **jocularly**[12] pass themselves off as Indians from Narragansett, since it's customary to blame the Indians for any lawless acts. They carry hatchets, described as tomahawks, as well as clubs, and some have painted their faces and hands with coal dust in a blacksmith shop, looking more like slaves than Indians.

Reaching the wharves, Pitts as leader divides the party into three groups, one for each ship, and leads his own group to the *Dartmouth,* where he sends a note to the mate, with a peremptory demand for the keys and a light to illuminate the dark hold. Without a word, the keys are forthcoming, a cabin boy brings lights, and the "Indians" go to work. They bring up the chests of tea to

---

[11] Author Tebbel says Molineux is an "enforcer" who leads a "gang of toughs" or "ruffians."

[12] **jocularly**—jokingly.

the deck, break them open, and throw the contents into the harbor. Similar scenes are taking place on the other two ships. At the moment, the tide is low, but when it rises again a windrow of tea will stretch from Boston to Dorchester.

Earlier suspicions prove justified. There are those who attempt to scoop up and conceal a little tea for themselves; they are dealt with quietly and severely. On the dock, thousands of people stand in a strange silence, watching the men at work. They had begun late in the evening, and before dawn they're finished; some claim it took only three hours. To the surprise of these **fraudulent**[13] Narragansetts, not a hand is raised against them, not a protest is heard. They come off the ships, form in a rude column, and with fife and drum preceding them, march to the State House.

One of the interested spectators of the unloading has been Admiral Montague,[14] commander of the British warships at Castle William, spending the night with a Tory friend whose house is so close to the wharf that the admiral is able to watch the whole affair from a window. As the Tea Party marches by, Montague has the **temerity**[15] to put his head out the window and shouts "Well, boys, you've had a fine, pleasant evening for your Indian capers, haven't you? But mind you, you've got to pay the fiddler yet."

"Never mind, squire," Lendell Pitts shouts back, "just come out here, if you please, and we'll settle the bill in two minutes." Prudently, the admiral retreats, and he's lucky that nothing worse happens to him.

At the State House, the Party huzzahs[16] and disperses. Betsy Hunt Palmer reports later that she was rocking her baby that dawning when the parlor door opened

---

[13] **fraudulent**—fake.

[14] Admiral Montague—British statesman; Prime Minister from 1714–1715.

[15] **temerity**—reckless boldness.

[16] huzzahs—gives shouts of joy.

and "three stout Indians," one of whom was her husband, walked in. Before she could jump up, her husband said, "Don't be frightened, Betsy, it's I. We've only been making a little saltwater tea." But when George Hewes comes home, his wife Sally, a confirmed tea drinker, comes directly to the point: "Well, George, did you bring me home a lot of it?" Another of the conspirators, Thomas Melville, when he reaches his house and undresses, discovers that his shoes are full of tea. Thinking of posterity and the historic event he has just helped to create, he pours it into a glass bottle, labels, and seals it. The tea survives well into this century.

But Admiral Montague was right. The piper will have to be paid, and Hutchinson is about to make the first payment. He's absolutely stunned by what's happened that night. As a conservative, law-abiding man of principle, no matter what others may think, it's simply incomprehensible to him that such valuable property would be so ruthlessly sacrificed by men who obviously care nothing for the law or for property. Why, he wonders, would men like Hancock and his merchant friends be willing to pay for the tea they've destroyed—it doesn't occur to him that they would do otherwise—rather than pay the duty, which would have been much less.

As for his own responsibility, he stands as always on principle and the law. If he'd given in to this "lawless and highly criminal assembly," he says, he would have aided and abetted gross violation of the law. On the other hand, he can hardly escape some responsibility for the Tea Party. After all, he had been responsible for the protection of this valuable property, as well as for enforcing the revenue laws, and in both cases he has failed. When news of this event reaches London, he can confidently expect to be the ex-governor of Massachusetts, and that's exactly what occurs. But the piper will exact a far heavier payment from the

Bostonians. Parliament enacts what are called the Coercive Acts, and to enforce them, they appoint General Gage as the military governor of Massachusetts and give him what amounts to eleven regiments as insurance that the acts will be enforced.

QUESTIONS TO CONSIDER

1. Why are the colonists angry about the tea?

2. Is Hutchinson a wise or foolish governor? Explain your opinion.

3. Was the Boston Tea Party a heroic act of patriotism? Explain your thinking.

Speech to the Virginia Convention

BY PATRICK HENRY

Patrick Henry was a lawyer in the Virginia Colony and a fervent patriot. He was powerfully skilled in the art of persuasion. Some historians call him a "firebrand" or "rabble-rouser" because his strong language stirred the passions in crowds and encouraged violence. Others see him as a hero in the cause for freedom. In this, his most famous speech, he argued that the time had come to take up arms and fight against England. Later, when the nation was debating the need for a stronger government than the Articles of Confederation provided, he would be an Antifederalist—again arguing against the restraints on freedom a powerful government can impose.

This is no time for ceremony. The question before the house is one of awful moment to this country. For my own part, I consider it as nothing less than a question of freedom or slavery. And in proportion to the magnitude of the subject ought to be the freedom of the debate. It is only in this way that we can hope to arrive at the truth, and fulfill the great responsibility which we hold to God and our country. Should I keep back my opinions at such a time, through fear of giving offense, I should consider myself as guilty of treason towards my country, and of an act of disloyalty toward the Majesty of Heaven, which I revere above all earthly kings.

Mr. President, it is natural to man to indulge in the illusions of hope. We are apt to shut our eyes against a painful truth, and listen to the song of that siren[1] till she transforms us into beasts. Is this the part of wise men, engaged in a great and arduous struggle for liberty? Are we disposed to be of the numbers of those who, having eyes, see not, and, having ears, hear not, the things which so nearly concern their temporal salvation? For my part, whatever anguish of spirit it may cost, I am willing to know the whole truth, to know the worst, and to provide for it.

I have but one lamp by which my feet are guided, and that is the lamp of experience. I know of no way of judging of the future but by the past. And judging by the past, I wish to know what there has been in the conduct of the British ministry for the last ten years to justify those hopes with which gentlemen have been pleased to solace themselves and the House. Is it that insidious smile with which our petition has been lately received? Trust it not, sir; it will prove a snare to your feet. Suffer not yourselves to be betrayed with a kiss.

Ask yourselves how this gracious reception of our petition **comports**[2] with those warlike preparations which cover our waters and darken our land. Are fleets and armies necessary to a work of love and reconciliation? Have we shown ourselves so unwilling to be reconciled that force must be called in to win back our

---

[1] song of that siren—in Greek mythology, the Sirens sang melodies so beautiful that sailors passing their rocky island were lured to shipwreck and death.

[2] **comports**—agrees.

love? Let us not deceive ourselves, sir. These are the implements of war and **subjugation**[3]—the last arguments to which kings resort.

I ask gentlemen, sir, what means this martial array, if its purpose be not to force us to submission? Can gentlemen assign any other possible motive for it? Has Great Britain any enemy, in this quarter of the world, to call for all this accumulation of navies and armies? No, sir, she has none. They are meant for us: they can be meant for no other. They are sent over to bind and rivet upon us those chains which the British ministry have been so long forging. And what have we to oppose to them? Shall we try argument? Sir, we have been trying that for the last ten years. Have we anything new to offer upon the subject? Nothing. We have held the subject up in every light of which it is capable; but it has been all in vain. Shall we resort to entreaty and humble supplication? What terms shall we find which have not been already exhausted? Let us not, I beseech you, sir, deceive ourselves longer. Sir, we have done everything that could be done to avert the storm which is now coming on. We have petitioned—we have **remonstrated**[4]— we have **supplicated**[5]—we have **prostrated**[6] ourselves before the throne, and have implored its **interposition**[7] to arrest the tyrannical hands of the ministry and Parliament. Our petitions have been slighted; our remonstrances have produced additional violence and insult; our supplications have been disregarded; and we have been spurned, with contempt, from the foot of the throne.

In vain, after these things, may we indulge the fond hope of peace and reconciliation.

---

[3] **subjugation**—dominance, humiliation.

[4] **remonstrated**—pleaded in protest.

[5] **supplicated**—asked for humbly; beseeched.

[6] **prostrated**—bowed or kneeled down in humility.

[7] **interposition**—intervention.

There is no longer any room for hope. If we wish to be free—if we mean to preserve **inviolate**[8] those inestimable privileges for which we have been so long contending—if we mean not basely to abandon the noble struggle in which we have been so long engaged, and which we have pledged ourselves never to abandon until the glorious object of our contest shall be obtained—we must fight! I repeat it, sir, we must fight! An appeal to arms and to the God of hosts is all that is left us!

They tell us, sir, that we are weak—unable to cope with so formidable an adversary. But when shall we be stronger? Will it be the next week, or the next year? Will it be when we are totally disarmed, and when a British guard shall be stationed in every house? Shall we gather strength by irresolution and inaction? Shall we acquire the means of effectual resistance by lying **supinely**[9] on our backs and hugging the **delusive**[10] phantom of hope, until our enemies shall have bound us hand and foot? Sir, we are not weak if we make a proper use of those means which the God of nature hath placed in our power.

Three millions of people, armed in the holy cause of liberty, and in such a country as that which we possess, are invincible by any force which our enemy can send against us. Besides, sir, we shall not fight our battles alone. There is a just God who presides over the destinies of nations, and who will raise up friends to fight our battles for us. The battle, sir, is not to the strong alone; it is to the vigilant, the active, the brave. Besides, sir, we have no election. If we were base enough to desire it, it is now too late to retire from the contest. There is no retreat but in submission and slavery! Our chains are forged! Their clanking may be heard on the

---

[8] **inviolate**—unbroken.

[9] **supinely**—passively.

[10] **delusive**—deceptive.

plains of Boston! The war is inevitable—and let it come! I repeat it, sir, let it come!

It is in vain, sir, to **extenuate**[11] the matter. Gentlemen may cry, Peace, Peace—but there is no peace. The war is actually begun! The next gale that sweeps from the north will bring to our ears the clash of resounding arms! Our brethren are already in the field! Why stand we here idle? What is it that gentlemen wish? What would they have? Is life so dear, or peace so sweet, as to be purchased at the price of chains and slavery? Forbid it, Almighty God!—I know not what course others may take; but as for me, give me liberty or give me death!

---

[11] **extenuate**—lessen or attempt to lessen the seriousness of.

QUESTIONS TO CONSIDER

1. Is Patrick Henry concerned that England might be too powerful an adversary for the colonies? Why or why not?

2. Why does Patrick Henry conclude that there is no hope for a peaceful resolution of the conflict with Britain?

3. What would you say are Patrick Henry's top two or three reasons for arguing that the colonists should take up arms?

Colonial Defiance

▲

King George III Britain's king believes that the American colonists should pay their share of the costs of their defense. When Parliament passes the Stamp Act, he supports it.

Anno Regni

GEORGII III.

R E G I S

Magnæ Britanniæ, Franciæ, & Hiberniæ,

Q U I N T O.

At the Parliament begun and holden at *Weftmin-ſter*, the Nineteenth Day of *May, Anno Dom.* 1761, in the Firſt Year of the Reign of our Sovereign Lord *GEORGE* the Third, by the Grace of God, of *Great Britain*, *France*, and *Ireland*, King, Defender of the Faith, *&c.*

And from thence continued by ſeveral Prorogations to the Tenth Day of *January*, 1765, being the Fourth Seſſion of the Twelfth Parliament of *Great Britain*.

L O N D O N:

Printed by *Mark Baſkett*, Printer to the King's moſt Excellent Majeſty; and by the Aſſigns of *Robert Baſkett*. 1765.

The·TIMES are
Dreadful,
Dismal,
Doleful,
Dolorous, and
DOLLAR-LESS.

of the STAMP

An Emblem of the Effects

O! the fatal Stamp

Thursday, *October* 31, 1765.   NUMB 1195.

THE
PENNSYLVANIA JOURNAL;
AND
WEEKLY ADVERTISER.

EXPIRING: In Hopes of a Resurrection to LIFE again.

I

AM forry to be obliged to acquaint my Readers, that as The STAMP. Act, is fear'd to be obligatory upon us after the First of November enfuing, (the fatal To morrow) the Publisher of this Paper unable to bear the Burthen, has thought it expedient to stop awhile, in order to deliberate, whether any Methods can be found to elude the Chains forged for us, and escape the insupportable Slavery, which it is hoped, from the last Representations now made against that Act, may be effected. Mean while, I must earnestly Request every Individual of my Subfcribers, many of whom have been long behind Hand, that they would immediately Discharge their refpective Arrears that I may be able, not only to support myself during the Interval, but be better prepared to proceed again with this Paper, whenever an opening for that Purpose appears, which I hope will be foon.   WILLIAM BRADFORD

▲

The Stamp Act Taxes Newspapers The editors of the *Pennsylvania Journal* put a skull and crossbones in a square on the right of its masthead to show where the tax stamp should be affixed. The words around it say: "An Emblem of the Effects of the Stamp. O! the fatal Stamp." On the left it says, "The TIMES are Dreadful, Dismal, Doleful, Dolorous, and DOLLAR-LESS."

◄ **Stamp Act** The title page of the first edition of the Stamp Act, 1765.

The British tax stamp as it would have been used on the *Pennsylvania Journal.*
▼

NUMB. 1195.

OURNAL;

TISER.

to LIFE again.

▲

Patrick Henry The 29-year-old lawyer introduces resolutions against the tax in the Virginia legislature. Virginians can only be taxed by their own representatives, he says. The resolutions pass.

◄ **Tarring and Feathering of John Malcolm** Colonists tar and feather a tax collector. This drawing in a French news report pictures an incident in January 1774.

Boston Tea Party The accompanying caption reads: "Americans throwing the Cargoes of the Tea Ships into the River at Boston."
▼

▲

Patriot Propaganda Paul Revere took liberties with the facts when he engraved this illustration for the *Boston Gazette*.

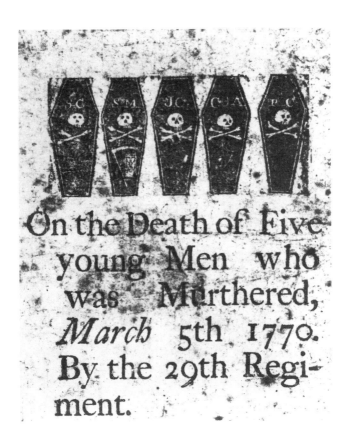

▲
Patriot Propaganda The poster with coffins says: "On the Death of Five young Men who was Murthered, March 5th, 1770. By the 29th Regiment."

▲

Paul Revere calls out the Minutemen British General Gage and his troops are marching from Boston to Concord to seize the Patriots' weapons. The signal goes from town to town, "The British are coming!" ▶

"A LIST of the Names of the PROVINCIALS who were Killed and Wounded in the late Engagement with His Majesty's Troops at *Concord.*" ▶

Victory for the Colonists! After brief battles at Lexington and Concord, the British march back to Boston. All along the way, Minutemen fire on them from behind stone walls and from barns. In Boston, the Minutemen lay siege to the town and confine the British there.
▼

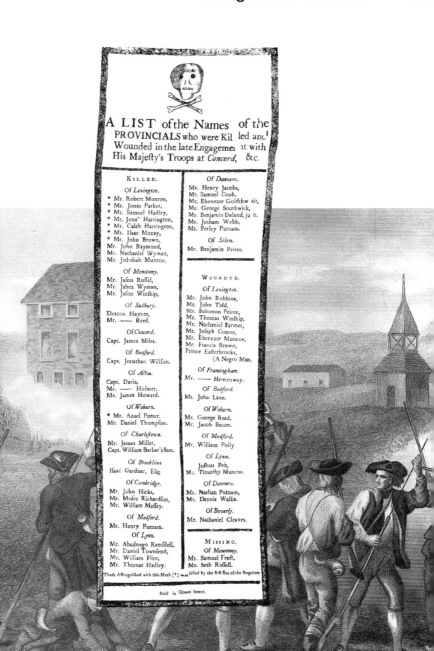

"View of the attack on Bunker's Hill, with the burning of Charles Town, June 17, 1775."

▼

BOSTON

▲
"A Real American Rifle Man."

Revolution
Begins

Declaration of Taking Up Arms

BY THE SECOND CONTINENTAL CONGRESS

On July 6, 1775, a year before the Declaration of Independence, the Second Continental Congress concluded that the colonies must arm themselves against Great Britain. It was important to the delegates that other nations, such as France, understood their reasons. They hoped that France, a recent enemy of Britain, would support their cause. However, France also had colonies, and the delegates wanted to assure France that it was not colonialism they were against, but Britain. The following declaration contains their justification.

A declaration by the representatives of the United Colonies of North America, now met in general Congress at Philadelphia, setting forth the causes and necessity of their taking up arms. . . .

Our forefathers, inhabitants of the island of Great Britain, left their native land to seek on these shores a residence for civil and religious freedom. At the expense of their blood, at the hazard of their fortunes, without the least charge to the country from which they removed, by unceasing labor, and an unconquerable spirit, they effected settlements in the distant and inhospitable wilds of America, then filled with numerous and warlike nations of barbarians. Societies or governments, vested with perfect legislatures, were formed under charters from the crown, and a harmonious intercourse was established between the colonies and the kingdom from which they derived their origin. The mutual benefits of this union became in a short time so extraordinary as to excite astonishment. It is universally confessed that the amazing increase of the wealth, strength, and navigation of the realm arose from this source; and the minister, who so wisely and successfully directed the measures of Great Britain in the late war, publicly declared that these colonies enabled her to triumph over her enemies.

Toward the conclusion of that war, it pleased our sovereign to make a change in his counsels. From that fatal moment, the affairs of the British Empire began to fall into confusion. . . . The new ministry finding the brave foes of Britain, though frequently defeated, yet still contending, took up the unfortunate idea of granting them a hasty peace and of then subduing her faithful friends.

These devoted colonies were judged to be in such a state, as to present victories without bloodshed, and all the easy **emoluments**[1] of statutable **plunder**[2]. . . .

In the course of eleven years, [Parliament has] . . . undertaken to give and grant our money without our consent, though we have ever exercised an exclusive right to dispose of our own property; statutes have been passed for extending the jurisdiction of courts of admiralty and vice-admiralty beyond their ancient limits; for

---

[1] **emoluments**—compensation.

[2] **plunder**—property stolen by force; booty.

depriving us of the accustomed and inestimable privilege of trial by jury, in cases affecting both life and property; for suspending the legislature of one of the colonies; for interdicting all commerce to the capital of another; and for altering fundamentally the form of government established by charter and secured by acts of its own legislature solemnly confirmed by the crown; for exempting the "murderers" of colonists from legal trial and, in effect, from punishment; for erecting in a neighboring province, acquired by the joint arms of Great Britain and America, a despotism dangerous to our very existence; and for quartering soldiers upon the colonists in time of profound peace. It has also been resolved in Parliament that colonists charged with committing certain offenses shall be transported to England to be tried. . . .

We for ten years incessantly and ineffectually besieged the throne as **supplicants;**[3] we reasoned, we remonstrated with Parliament, in the most mild and decent language. . . .

The indignation of the Americans was roused, it is true; but it was the indignation of a virtuous, loyal, and affectionate people. A Congress of Delegates from the United Colonies was assembled at Philadelphia, on the fifth day of last September. We resolved again to offer a humble and dutiful petition to the king, and also addressed our fellow-subjects of Great Britain. We have pursued every temperate, every respectful, measure. . . . But subsequent events have shown how vain was this hope of finding moderation in our enemies.

Several threatening expressions against the colonies were inserted in His Majesty's speech; our petition, though we were told it was a decent one, and that His Majesty had been pleased to receive it graciously, and to promise laying it before his Parliament, was huddled into both houses amongst a bundle of American papers, and there neglected.

---

[3] **supplicants**—those who make a humble entreaty.

The Lords and Commons in their address, in the month of February, said, that "a rebellion at that time actually existed within the province of Massachusetts Bay; and that those concerned in it, had been countenanced and encouraged by unlawful combinations and engagements, entered into by His Majesty's subjects in several of the other colonies; and therefore they **besought**[4] His Majesty, that he would take the most effectual measures to enforce due obedience to the laws and authority of the supreme legislature."

Soon after, the commercial intercourse of whole colonies, with foreign countries, and with each other, was cut off by an act of Parliament; by another, several of them were entirely prohibited from the fisheries in the seas near their coasts, on which they always depended for their sustenance; and large reinforcements of ships and troops were immediately sent over to General Gage. . . .

Soon after the intelligence of these proceedings arrived on this continent, General Gage, who in the course of the last year had taken possession of the town of Boston, in the province of Massachusetts Bay, and still occupied it as a garrison, on the 19th day of April, sent out from that place a large detachment of his army, who made an unprovoked assault on the inhabitants of the said province, at the town of Lexington . . . [and] murdered eight of the inhabitants, and wounded many others.

From thence the troops proceeded in warlike array to the town of Concord, where they set upon another party of the inhabitants of the same province, killing several and wounding more, until compelled to retreat by the country people suddenly assembled to repel this cruel aggression.

Hostilities, thus commenced by the British troops, have been since prosecuted by them without regard to

---

[4] **besought**—begged; beseeched.

faith or reputation. The inhabitants of Boston being confined within that town by the General, their Governor, [who] . . . ordered the arms . . . be seized by a body of soldiers; detained the greatest part of the inhabitants in the town, and compelled the few who were permitted to retire to leave their most valuable effects behind.

By this **perfidy**[5] wives are separated from their husbands, children from their parents, the aged and the sick from their relations and friends, who wish to attend and comfort them; and those who have been used to live in plenty and even elegance are reduced to deplorable distress.

The General further [declared] . . . the good people of these colonies . . . to be rebels and traitors. . . . His troops have butchered our countrymen, have wantonly burned Charles-Town, besides a considerable number of houses in other places; our ships and vessels are seized; the necessary supplies of provisions are intercepted, and he is exerting his utmost power to spread destruction and devastation around him.

We have received certain intelligence that General Carleton, the Governor of Canada, is instigating the people of that province and the Indians to fall upon us; and we have but too much reason to apprehend that schemes have been formed to excite domestic enemies against us. . . . We are reduced to the alternative of choosing an unconditional submission to the tyranny of irritated ministers, or resistance by force. The latter is our choice. . . .

Our cause is just. Our union is perfect. Our internal resources are great, and, if necessary, foreign assistance is undoubtedly attainable. . . .

Lest this declaration should disquiet the minds of our friends and fellow-subjects in any part of the Empire, we assure them that we mean not to dissolve

---

[5] **perfidy**—disloyalty; treachery.

that union which has so long and so happily subsisted between us, and which we sincerely wish to see restored. Necessity has not yet driven us into that desperate measure, or induced us to excite any other nation to war against them. We have not raised armies with ambitious designs of separating from Great Britain and establishing independent states. We fight not for glory or for conquest. We exhibit to mankind the remarkable spectacle of a people attacked by unprovoked enemies, without any imputation or even suspicion of offense. They boast of their privileges and civilization and yet proffer no milder conditions than servitude or death.

In our own native land, in defense of the freedom that is our birthright, and which we ever enjoyed till the late violation of it—for the protection of our property, acquired solely by the honest industry of our forefathers and ourselves, against violence actually offered, we have taken up arms. We shall lay them down when hostilities shall cease on the part of the aggressors, and all danger of their being renewed shall be removed, and not before.

With a humble confidence in the mercies of the supreme and impartial Judge and Ruler of the universe, we most devoutly implore his divine goodness to protect us happily through this great conflict, to dispose our adversaries to reconciliation on reasonable terms, and thereby to relieve the Empire from the calamities of civil war.

By order of Congress,
JOHN HANCOCK,
President

Attested,
CHARLES THOMSON,
Secretary
PHILADELPHIA, July 6th, 1775

QUESTIONS TO CONSIDER

1. What is the purpose of the "Declaration of Taking Up Arms"?

2. According to Hancock, are the colonists eager or reluctant to go to war? How do you know?

3. Does John Hancock make a strong case for the colonies? Explain your opinion.

A Plea to the Continental Congress

BY GENERAL GEORGE WASHINGTON

In September 1775, the militiamen had been holding Boston under siege since the Battle at Concord in April. The Second Continental Congress had recognized them officially as the Continental Army and put George Washington over them. But the delegates had limited resources and were not sure how much power to give to him. Meanwhile, the troops had signed on for only a short time. Many would be able to go home at the end of the year, and they were already declaring they would do so. Washington wrote of his concerns to the Congress, who appointed a committee, headed by Benjamin Franklin. The committee met with Washington in his headquarters at Cambridge, outside Boston. He was given approval to call out the New England militia, and plans were drawn up to get him money. Here is how Washington described the army's plight.

It gives me great pain to be obliged to solicit the attention of the honourable Congress to the state of this army in terms which imply the slightest apprehension of being neglected. But my situation is inexpressibly distressing, to see the winter fast approaching upon a naked army, the time of their service within a few weeks of expiring, and no provision yet made for such important events. Added to these, the military chest is totally exhausted. The paymaster has not a single dollar in hand. The commissary-general, he assures me, has strained his credit for the subsistence of the army to the utmost. The quartermaster-general is precisely in the same situation; and the greater part of the troops are in a state not far from mutiny [because of] the deduction from their stated allowance. I know not to whom I am to **impute**[1] this failure; but I am of [the] opinion, if the evil is not immediately remedied, and more punctuality observed in the future, the army must absolutely break up.

---

[1] **impute**—blame for.

QUESTIONS TO CONSIDER

1. What is the purpose of General Washington's letter?

2. Why can't the army buy new uniforms?

3. What is Washington's tone in his letter?

Attacks on Loyalists

FROM NEWSPAPER ARTICLES AND JOURNALS

This selection, from Richard Wheeler's Voices of 1776, tells of the friction between Patriots and Loyalists late in 1775.

In November 1775, the colony of New York was the scene of a mob action that won widespread Patriot applause, since its chief accomplishment was the silencing of an influential Loyalist press. As narrated by the Pennsylvania Journal:

On the twentieth of this month, sixteen respectable inhabitants of New Haven, Connecticut, in company with Captain Sears, set out from that place to East and West Chester, in the province of New York, to disarm the principal Tories[1] there and secure the persons of Parson Seabury, Judge Fowler and Lord Underhill. On their way thither they were joined by Captains Richards, Sillick and Mead, with about eighty men.

---

[1] Tories—the Loyalists, those who supported the British government and opposed separation from Britain.

At Mamaroneck they burnt a small **sloop**[2] which was
. . . [used] for the purpose of carrying provisions on
board the Asia. At East Chester they seized Judge
Fowler, then repaired to West Chester and secured
Seabury and Underhill. Having possessed themselves
of these three **caitiffs,**[3] they sent them to Connecticut
under a strong guard.

The main body, consisting of seventy-five, then proceeded to New York, where they entered at noonday on
horseback, bayonets fixed, in the greatest regularity,
went down the main street and drew up in close order
before the printing office of the infamous James
Rivington. A small detachment entered it, and in about
three-quarters of an hour brought off the principal part
of his types [having smashed his presses]. . . . They then
faced and wheeled to the left and marched out of town
to the tune of Yankee Doodle. A vast concourse of people assembled at the Coffee House, on their leaving the
ground, and gave them three very hearty cheers.

On their way home they disarmed all the Tories
that lay on their route, and yesterday arrived at New
Haven escorted by a great number of gentlemen from
the westward, the whole making a very grand procession. Upon their entrance into town they were saluted
with the discharge of two cannon and received by the
inhabitants with every mark of **approbation**[4] and
respect. The company divided into two parts and concluded the day in festivity and innocent mirth. . . .
Seabury, Underhill and Fowler, three of the **dastardly**[5]
protesters against the proceedings of the Continental
Congress, and who it is believed had concerted a plan
for kidnapping Captain Sears and conveying him on

---

[2] **sloop**—sailboat.

[3] **caitiffs**—despicable cowards.

[4] **approbation**—approval.

[5] **dastardly**—cowardly and malicious.

board the Asia man-of-war,[6] are . . . safely lodged in New Haven. . . .

Loyalist Judge Jones adds angrily:
. . . they were all confined in a public house under a strict guard, where every low-lived wretch for ten miles around the country had free liberty to enter their apartments at pleasure and to treat them with the vilest language, accusing them as enemies to their country, as the friends of a tyrant, and betrayers of the liberties of America. . . . These gentlemen, after being detained as prisoners for many weeks at a heavy expense to themselves (no provision being made for their maintenance) and absent from their business, their families, and avocations, were discharged and suffered to return home without the least compensation being made for the damages they sustained, and without being ever permitted to prosecute the persons by whom they had been robbed, plundered, **pillaged,**[7] insulted and imprisoned, for no other reason than acknowledging themselves (as they really were) the lawful subjects of the King of Great Britain.

An example of one of the commonest things done to professed Loyalists was noted in a December issue of the New York Journal:

At Quibbletown, New Jersey, Thomas Randolph, cooper, who had publicly proved himself an enemy to his country by **reviling**[8] and using his utmost endeavors to oppose the proceedings of the continental and provincial conventions in defence of their rights and liberties; and being judged a person not of consequence enough for a severer punishment, was ordered to be

---

[6] man-of-war—warship.
[7] **pillaged**—robbed of goods by force, usually by an attacking army.
[8] **reviling**—cursing; verbally attacking.

stripped naked, well coated with tar and feathers, and carried in a wagon publicly around the town—which punishment was accordingly inflicted. As soon as he became duly sensible of his offence, for which he earnestly begged pardon, and promised to atone as far as he was able by a contrary behavior for the future, he was released and suffered to return to his house in less than half an hour. The whole was conducted with that regularity and decorum that ought to be observed in all public punishments.

Not all of the Patriots approved of Tory persecution. Some, in fact, were deeply distressed by the practice. But no less a person than George Washington believed that the Tories had to be subdued: "Why should persons who are preying on the vitals of this country be suffered to stalk at large, whilst we know that they will do us every mischief in their power?"

There were, of course, Patriot women who joined the campaign against the Tories. A diarist of the day recorded:

The following droll affair lately happened at Kinderhook, New York. A young fellow, an enemy to the liberties of America, going to a quilting frolic where a number of young women were collected, and he the only man in company, began his **aspersions**[9] on Congress as usual, and held forth some time on the subject, till the girls, exasperated at his **impudence**,[10] laid hold of him, stripped him naked to the waist, and instead of tar, covered him with molasses, and for feathers took the downy tops of flags which grow in the meadows, and coated him well and then let him go.

---

[9] **aspersions**—slanders, damaging remarks.

[10] **impudence**—insolence; impertinence.

QUESTIONS TO CONSIDER

1. Who are the Patriots? Who are the Loyalists?

2. How does Washington feel about the practice of Tory persecution?

3. What do the actions of the Patriots—and the general public's reaction to these actions—suggest about the prevailing mood in the colonies and the status of the Second Continental Congress?

The Crisis Deepens

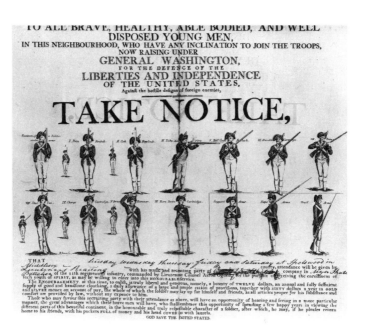

▲
Recruiting Poster The poster, issued in George Washington's name, offers men who enlist $12 to join, $60 a year in pay, and "the opportunity of spending a few happy years in viewing the different parts of this beautiful continent" and returning home "with. . . pockets full of money and. . . head COVERED with laurels."

◄ **George Washington** Charles Willson Peale painted this picture of Washington at Princeton in 1779.

Mocking the British In "British Heroism" (above), the King's troops are shown charging cows with their rifles. In "The Combat" (right), a small crowd cheers a farmer whose shovel is his only weapon against a pompous, wigged Loyalist.

A Declaration by the Representatives of the UNITED STATES
OF AMERICA, in General Congress assembled.

When in the course of human events it becomes necessary for one people to
dissolve the political bands which have connected them with another, and to as
-sume among the powers of the earth the separate and equal station to
which the laws of nature & of nature's god entitle them, a decent respect
to the opinions of mankind requires that they should declare the causes
which impel them to the separation.

We hold these truths to be self-evident; that all men are
created equal, that they are endowed by their creator with
inherent & inalienable rights; that among these are the preservation of
life, & liberty, & the pursuit of happiness; that to secure these rights, governments are instituted among men, deriving their just powers from
the consent of the governed; that whenever any form of government
becomes destructive of these ends, it is the right of the people to alter
or to abolish it, & to institute new government, laying it's foundation on
such principles & organising it's powers in such form, as to them shall
seem most likely to effect their safety & happiness. prudence indeed
will dictate that governments long established should not be changed for
light & transient causes: and accordingly all experience hath shewn that
mankind are more disposed to suffer while evils are sufferable than to
right themselves by abolishing the forms to which they are accustomed. but
when a long train of abuses & usurpations [begun at a distinguished period
&] pursuing invariably the same object, evinces a design to reduce
them under absolute Despotism, it is their right, it is their duty, to throw off such
government & to provide new guards for their future security. such has
been the patient sufferance of these colonies; & such is now the necessity
which constrains them to expunge their former systems of government.
the history of the present King of Great Britain is a history of unremitting injuries and
usurpations, among which appears no solitary fact to contra-
dict the uniform tenor of the rest, [all of which have] in direct object the
establishment of an absolute tyranny over these states. to prove this, let facts be
submitted to a candid world, [for the truth of which we pledge a faith
yet unsullied by falsehood.]

▲
The signing of the Declaration of Independence by painter John Trumbull.

◀ The first page of Jefferson's draft of the Declaration of Independence showing changes he made as he and the committee worked through it.

▲

Congress Voting on the Declaration of Independence An engraving by Edward

Hamilton delin.   Noble sculp.

▲
Colonists Cheer the News of the Declaration of Independence This
engraving carried the caption: "*The Manner in which the American Colonies
Declared themselves* INDEPENDENT *of the King of* ENGLAND, *throughout
the different Provinces on July 4, 1776.*"

Thomas Paine and *Common Sense*

BY BERNARD BAILYN

Ideas played a very important part in the founding of the nation. Ideas of the Enlightenment in Europe had earlier shaped people's thoughts about the relationship between people and their government. The words of powerful speakers such as Patrick Henry had stirred the flames of rebellion. Writers fanned the flames from the pages of the print media—a favorite being the pamphlet. The most important pamphlet of the time was Common Sense. *Here, from his book* Faces of Revolution, *Pulitzer Prize–winning historian Bernard Bailyn explains what it is that makes this extraordinary work so powerful.*

Thomas Paine's *Common Sense* is the most brilliant pamphlet written during the American Revolution, and one of the most brilliant pamphlets ever written in the English language. How it could have been produced by the bankrupt Quaker corset-maker, the some-time teacher, preacher, and grocer, and twice-dismissed excise officer[1] who happened to catch Benjamin Franklin's attention in England and who arrived in America only fourteen months before *Common Sense* was published is nothing one can explain without explaining genius itself. For it is a work of genius—slapdash as it is, rambling as it is, crude as it is. It "burst from the press," Benjamin Rush wrote, "with an effect which has rarely been produced by types and papers in any age or country." Its effect, Franklin said, was "prodigious." It touched some extraordinarily sensitive nerve in American political awareness in the confusing period in which it appeared.

It was written by an Englishman, not an American. Paine had only the barest acquaintance with American affairs when, with Rush's encouragement, he turned an invitation by Franklin to write a history of the Anglo-American controversy into the occasion for composing a passionate tract for American independence. Yet not only does *Common Sense* voice some of the deepest aspirations of the American people on the eve of the Revolution but it also evokes, with superb vigor and with perfect intonation, longings and aspirations that have remained part of American culture to this day. . . .

If it is an exaggeration, it is not much of an exaggeration to say that one had to be a fool or a fanatic in early January 1776 to advocate American independence. Militia troops may have been able to defend themselves at certain points and had achieved some limited goals, but the first extended military campaign was ending in a **squalid**[2] defeat below the walls of Quebec. There was no evidence of an area of agreement among the thirteen separate governments and among the hundreds of conflicting American interests that was broad enough and

---

[1] excise officer—tax official.

[2] **squalid**—wretched.

firm enough to support an effective common government. Everyone knew that England was the most powerful nation on earth, and if its navy had fallen into disrepair, it could be swiftly rebuilt. Anyone in whom common sense outweighed enthusiasm and imagination knew that a string of prosperous but weak communities along the Atlantic coast left uncontrolled and unprotected by England would quickly be pounced on by rival European powers, whose ruling political notions and whose institutions of government were the opposite of what Americans had been struggling to preserve. The most obvious presumption of all was that the liberties Americans sought were British in their nature: they had been achieved by Britain over the centuries and had been embedded in a constitution whose wonderfully contrived balance between the needs of the state and the rights of the individual was thought throughout the Western world to be one of the finest human achievements. It was obvious too, of course, that something had gone wrong recently. It was generally agreed in the colonies that the famous balance of the constitution, in Britain and America, had been thrown off by a gang of ministers greedy for power, and that their attention had been drawn to the colonies by the misrepresentations of certain colonial officeholders who hoped to find an open route to influence and fortune in the enlargement of Crown power in the colonies. But the British constitution had been under attack before, and although at certain junctures in the past drastic action had been necessary to reestablish the balance, no one of importance had ever concluded that the constitution itself was at fault; no one had ever cast doubt on the principle that liberty, as the colonists knew it, rested on—had in fact been created by—the stable balancing of the three essential socio-constitutional orders, the monarchy, the nobility, and the people at large, each with its appropriate organ of government: the Crown, the House of Lords, and the

House of Commons. If the balance had momentarily been thrown off, let Americans, like Britishers in former ages, fight to restore it: force the evildoers out, and recover the protection of the only system ever known to guarantee both liberty and order. America had flourished under that benign system, and it was simply common sense to try to restore its balance. Why should one want to destroy the most successful political system in the world, which had been constructed by generations of constitutional architects, each building on and refining the wisdom of his predecessors, simply because its present managers were vicious or criminal? And was it reasonable to think that these ill-coordinated, weak communities along the Atlantic coast could defeat England in war and then construct governments free of the defects that had been revealed in the almost perfect English system?

Since we know how it came out, these seem rather artificial and rhetorical questions. But in early January 1776 they were vital and urgent, and *Common Sense* was written to answer them. . . .

. . . many people, in Congress and out, had the memory of reading [*Common Sense*] as they accepted the final determination to move to independence. But, as John Adams noted, at least as many people were offended by the pamphlet as were persuaded by it—he himself later called it "a poor, ignorant, malicious, short-sighted, crapulous mass"—and we shall never know the proportions on either side with any precision.

What strikes one more forcefully now, at this distance in time, is something quite different from the question of the pamphlet's unmeasurable contribution to the movement toward independence. There is something extraordinary in this pamphlet and in the mind and imagination of the man who wrote it—something bizarre, outsized, unique—and that quality helps us understand, I believe, something essential in the Revolution as a whole.

Certainly the language is remarkable. For its prose alone, *Common Sense* would be a notable document—unique among the pamphlets of the American Revolution. Its phraseology is deeply involving—at times clever, at times outrageous, frequently startling in imagery and penetration—and becomes more vivid as the pamphlet progresses.

In the first substantive part of the pamphlet, **ostensibly**[3] an essay on the principles of government in general and of the English constitution in particular, the ideas are relatively abstract but the imagery is concrete: "Government, like dress, is the badge of lost innocence; the palaces of kings are built upon the ruins of the bowers of paradise." As for the "so much boasted constitution of England," it was "noble for the dark and slavish times in which it was erected"; but that was not really so remarkable, Paine said, for "when the world was overrun with tyranny, the least remove therefrom was a glorious rescue." In fact, Paine wrote, the British constitution is "imperfect, subject to convulsions, and incapable of producing what it seems to promise," all of which could be "easily demonstrated" to anyone who could shake himself loose from the fetters of prejudice. For "as a man who is attached to a prostitute is unfitted to choose or judge of a wife, so any prepossession in favour of a rotten constitution of government will disable us from discerning a good one."

The imagery becomes arresting in Part 2, on monarchy and hereditary succession, institutions which together, Paine wrote, formed "the most prosperous invention the devil ever set on foot for the promotion of idolatry." The heathens, who invented monarchy, at least had had the good sense to grant divinity only to their

---

[3] **ostensibly**—supposedly.

dead kings; "the Christian world hath improved on the plan by doing the same to their living ones. How impious is the title of sacred majesty applied to a worm, who in the midst of his splendor is crumbling into dust!" Hereditary right is ridiculed by nature herself, which so frequently gives "mankind an *ass for a lion.*"

What of the true origins of the present-day monarchs, so exalted by myth and supposedly sanctified by antiquity? In all probability, Paine wrote, the founder of any of the modern royal lines was "nothing better than the principal ruffian of some restless gang, whose savage manners or preeminence in subtilty, obtained him the title of chief among plunderers; and who, by increasing in power and extending his depredations, overawed the quiet and defenceless to purchase their safety by frequent contributions." The English monarchs? "No man in his senses can say that their claim under William the Conquerer is a very honourable one. A French bastard, landing with an armed banditti and establishing himself king of England against the consent of the natives, is in plain terms a very **paltry**[4] rascally original." Why should one even bother to explain the folly of hereditary right? It is said to provide continuity and hence to preserve a nation from civil wars. That, Paine said, is "the most bare-faced falsity ever imposed upon mankind." English history alone disproves it. There had been, Paine confidently declared, "no less than eight civil wars and nineteen rebellions" since the Conquest. The fact is that everywhere hereditary monarchy has "laid . . . the world in blood and ashes." "In England a king hath little more to do than to make war and give away places; which in plain terms is to impoverish the nation and set it together by the ears. A pretty business indeed for a man to be allowed eight hundred thousand sterling a year for, and worshipped into the

---

[4] **paltry**—trivial.

bargain!" People who are fools enough to believe the claptrap about monarchy, Paine wrote, should be allowed to do so without interference: "let them promiscuously worship the Ass and the Lion, and welcome."

But it is in the third section, "Thoughts on the Present State of American Affairs," that Paine's language becomes most effective and vivid. The emotional level is extremely high throughout these pages and the lyric passages even then must have seemed **prophetic:**[5]

> The sun never shined on a cause of greater worth. . . . 'Tis not the concern of a day, a year, or an age; posterity are virtually involved in the contest, and will be more or less affected even to the end of time by the proceedings now. Now is the seed-time of continental union, faith, and honour. The least fracture now will be like a name engraved with the point of a pin on the tender rind of a young oak; the wound will enlarge with the tree, and posterity read it in full grown characters.

The arguments in this section, proving the necessity for American independence and the colonies' capacity to achieve it, are elaborately worked out, and they respond to all the objections to independence that Paine had heard. But through all of these pages of argumentation, the prophetic, lyric note of the opening paragraphs continues to be heard, and a sense of urgency keeps the tension high. "Every thing that is right or reasonable," Paine writes, "pleads for separation. The blood of the slain, the weeping voice of nature cries, "'TIS TIME TO PART." *Now* is the time to act, he insists: "The present winter is worth an age if rightly employed, but if lost or neglected the whole continent will partake of the

---

[5] **prophetic**—like a prophet's vision of the future.

misfortune." The possibility of a peaceful conclusion to the controversy had vanished, "wherefore, since nothing but blows will do, for God's sake let us come to a final separation, and not leave the next generation to be cutting throats under the violated unmeaning names of parent and child." Not to act now would not eliminate the need for action, he wrote, but only postpone it to the next generation, which would clearly see that "a little more, a little further, would have rendered this continent the glory of the earth." To talk of reconciliation "with those in whom our reason forbids us to have faith, and our affections, wounded thro' a thousand pores, instruct us to detest, is madness and folly." The earlier harmony was irrecoverable: "Can ye give to prostitution its former innocence? Neither can ye reconcile Britain and America. . . . As well can the lover forgive the ravisher of his mistress as the continent forgive the murders of Britain." And the section ends with Paine's greatest **peroration:**[6]

> O ye that love mankind! Ye that dare to oppose not only the tyranny but the tyrant, stand forth! Every spot of the old world is overrun with oppression. Freedom hath been hunted round the globe. Asia and Africa have long expelled her. Europe regards her like a stranger, and England hath given her warning to depart. O! receive the fugitive, and prepare in time an asylum for mankind.

In the pamphlet literature of the American Revolution there is nothing comparable to this passage for sheer emotional intensity and lyric appeal. Its vividness must have leapt out of the pages to readers used to grayer, more **stolid**[7] prose.

---

[6] **peroration**—conclusion.

[7] **stolid**—dispassionate.

* * *

The dominant tone of *Common Sense* is that of rage. It was written by an enraged man—not someone who had reasoned doubts about the British constitution and the related establishment in America, but someone who hated them both and who wished to strike back at them in a savage response. The verbal surface of the pamphlet is heated, and it burned into the consciousness of contemporaries because below it was the flaming conviction, not simply that Britain was corrupt and that America should declare its independence, but that the whole of organized society and government was stupid and cruel and that it survived only because the atrocities it systematically imposed on humanity had been papered over with a veneer of mythology and superstition that numbed the mind and kept people from rising against the evils that oppressed them.

The aim of almost every other notable pamphlet of the Revolution—pamphlets written by lawyers, ministers, merchants, and planters—was to probe difficult, urgent, and controversial questions and make appropriate recommendations. Paine's aim was to tear the world apart—the world as it was known and as it was constituted. Paine had nothing of the close logic, scholarship, and rational tone of the best of the American pamphleteers. Paine was an ignoramus, both in ideas and in the practice of politics, next to Adams, Jefferson, Madison, or Wilson. He could not discipline his thoughts; they were sucked off continuously from the sketchy outline he apparently had in mind when he began the pamphlet, into the boiling vortex of his emotions. And he had none of the hard, quizzical, grainy quality of mind that led Madison to probe the deepest questions of republicanism not as an ideal contrast to monarchical corruption but as an operating, practical, everyday process of government capable of containing within it the explosive forces of society. Paine's writing was not meant to probe unknown realities of a future way of life, or to convince, or to explain; it was meant to overwhelm and destroy.

QUESTIONS TO CONSIDER

1. What does Paine say about the origins of the British monarchy?

2. What does Paine mean when he says, "Freedom hath been hunted round the globe"?

3. What is the tone of *Common Sense?*

4. Bailyn says that *Common Sense* was the most brilliant pamphlet of the Revolutionary period. He also states that Paine was an "ignoramus." Why does the author not view these two statements as a contradiction?

Letters

BY ABIGAIL AND JOHN ADAMS

Two of the most interesting figures of the American Revolution were John and Abigail Adams. He was a lawyer, a constitution writer, protester of the Stamp Act, and a defender of the British troops accused of murder in the Boston Massacre. Later, he was to become the second President of the United States. She was a brilliant letter-writer, keen observer of people and politics, and the mother of four children—one of whom would become the sixth President. Their marriage was hailed for its attributes of mutual respect and support. He was often described as short, bad-tempered, and proud; she, as witty and intelligent. Here, Abigail Adams shares some thoughts on what is going on while her husband is away at the Continental Congress in Philadelphia in the spring of 1776.

Abigail to John

I have nothing new to entertain you with, unless it be an account of a new set of nobility, which has lately taken the lead in Boston. You must know that there is a great scarcity of sugar and coffee, articles which the female part of the state is very loath to give up, especially whilst they consider the scarcity occasioned by the merchants having secreted a large quantity. There had been much **rout**[1] and noise in town for several weeks. Some stores had been opened by a number of people, and the coffee and sugar carried into the market and dealt out by pounds.

It is rumored that an eminent, wealthy, stingy merchant [Thomas Boylston] (also a bachelor) had a hogshead[2] of coffee in his store, which he refused to sell to the committee under six shillings per pound. A number of females—some say a hundred, some say more—assembled with a cart and trucks, marched down to the warehouse and demanded the keys, which he refused to deliver. Upon which one of them seized him by his neck, and tossed him into the cart. Upon his finding no quarter,[3] he delivered the keys, when they tipped up the cart and discharged him, then opened up the warehouse, hoisted out the coffee themselves, put it into the trucks and drove off.

2 March 1776.

I was greatly rejoiced at the return of your servant, to find you had safely arrived [in Philadelphia], and that you were well. . . . I am charmed with the sentiments of *Common Sense*, and wonder how an honest heart, one who wishes the welfare of his country and the happiness of posterity, can hesitate one moment at adopting them. I want to know how these sentiments are received in

---

[1] **rout**—public disturbance.

[2] hogshead—a large barrel or cask.

[3] quarter—mercy or clemency, especially when displayed or given to an enemy.

Congress. I dare say there would be no difficulty in procuring a vote and instructions from all the assemblies in New England for independence. I most sincerely wish that now, in the lucky moment [before war], it might be done.

March 31, 1776.

I long to hear that you have declared an independency and, by the way, in the new code of laws, which I suppose it will be necessary for you to make, I desire you would remember the ladies, and be more generous and favorable to them than [were] your ancestors. Do not put such unlimited power into the hands of the husbands. Remember all men would be tyrants if they could. If particular care and attention is not paid to the ladies, we are determined to [instigate] a rebellion, and will not hold ourselves bound by any laws in which we have no voice or representation.

That your sex are naturally tyrannical is a truth so thoroughly established as to admit of no dispute. But such of you as wish to be happy willingly give up the harsh title of master for the more tender and endearing one of friend. Why, then, not put it out of the power of the vicious and the lawless to use us with cruelty and indignity . . . ? Men of sense in all ages **abhor**[4] those customs which treat us only as the vassals of your sex. Regard us then as beings, placed by providence under your protection, and in imitation of the Supreme Being make use of that power only for our happiness.

---

[4] **abhor**—regard with horror or loathing.

John to Abigail
April 14, 1776.

As to your extraordinary code of laws, I cannot but laugh. We have been told that our struggle has loosened the bands of government everywhere. That children and apprentices were disobedient—that schools and colleges were grown turbulent—that Indians slighted their guardians and Negroes grew insolent to their masters. But your letter was the first intimation that another tribe more numerous and powerful than all the rest [had] grown discontented. This is rather too coarse a compliment, but you are so **saucy**,[5] I won't blot it out.

Depend upon it, we know better than to repeal our masculine systems. Although they are in full force, you know they are little more than theory. We dare not exert our power in its full latitude. We are obliged to go fair and softly, and, in practice, you know, we are the subjects. We have only the name of masters, and rather than give up this, which would completely subject us to the despotism of the petticoat, I hope General Washington, and all our brave heroes would fight. . . . A fine story, indeed. I begin to think the ministry as deep as they are wicked. After stirring up Tories, landjobbers, trimmers, bigots, Canadians, Indians, Negroes, Hanoverians, Hessians, Russians, Irish Roman Catholics, Scotch . . . at last they have stimulated the [women] to demand new privileges and [to] threaten to rebel.

---

[5] **saucy**—impertinent in an entertaining way; impossible to repress or control.

Abigail to John
May 7, 1776.

I cannot say that I think you very generous to the ladies. For, whilst you are proclaiming peace and good will to men, emancipating all nations, you insist upon retaining an absolute power over wives. But you must remember that arbitrary power is like most other things which are very hard—very liable to be broken; and, notwithstanding all your wise laws and **maxims**,[6] we have it in our power not only to free ourselves but to subdue our masters, and without violence throw both your natural and legal authority at our feet.

---

[6] **maxims**—statements of fundamental principles, general truths, or rules of conduct.

QUESTIONS TO CONSIDER

1. What request does Abigail make of her husband in her letter of March 31?

2. How does John Adams respond to her request?

3. How would you describe John and Abigail's relationship?

Writing the Declaration of Independence

BY JOHN ADAMS

For months, the delegates to the Second Continental Congress had been locked in a heated debate. Should the Congress declare independence from Great Britain, or do the delegates need the approval of the voters in the states they represent? Public sentiment was growing, and by June 7, 1776, Richard Henry Lee made a motion for independence. On July 2 the delegates approved the motion, and a small committee was appointed to write a document. The group included John Adams and Thomas Jefferson, the youngest delegate. Here, John Adams explains why they chose him.

You inquire why so young a man as Mr. Jefferson was placed at the head of the committee for preparing a Declaration of Independence? I answer: It was the Frankfort advice to place Virginia at the head of everything.

Mr. Jefferson came into Congress in June, 1775, and brought with him a reputation for literature, science, and a happy talent of composition. Writings of his were handed about, remarkable for the peculiar **felicity**[1] of expression. Though a silent member in Congress, he was so prompt, frank, explicit and decisive upon committees and in conversation—not even Samuel Adams was more so—that he soon seized upon my heart; and upon this occasion I gave him my vote, and did all in my power to procure the votes of others.

I think he had one more vote than any other, and that placed him at the head of the committee. I had the next highest number, and that placed me the second. The committee . . . appointed Mr. Jefferson and me to make the [draft], I suppose because we were the two first. . . .

Jefferson proposed to me to make the [draft].

I said, "I will not."

"You should do it."

"Oh, no!"

"Why will you not? You ought to do it."

"I will not."

"Why?"

"Reason enough."

"What can be your reasons?"

"Reason first—You are a Virginian, and a Virginian ought to appear at the head of this business. Reason second—I am obnoxious, suspected and unpopular. You are very much otherwise. Reason third—You can write ten times better than I can."

"Well," said Jefferson, "if you are decided, I will do as well as I can."

---

[1] **felicity**—pleasing manner or quality.

"Very well. When you have drawn it up, we will have a meeting."

A meeting we accordingly had, and **conned**[2] the paper over. I was delighted with its high tone and the flights of oratory with which it abounded, especially that concerning Negro slavery, which, though I knew his Southern brethren would never suffer to pass in Congress, I certainly never would oppose.

There were other expressions which I would not have inserted . . . particularly that which called the King tyrant. I thought this too personal; for I never believed George to be a tyrant in disposition and in nature; I always believed him to be deceived by his **courtiers**[3] on both sides of the Atlantic. . . . I consented to report it [the Declaration], and do not now remember that I made . . . a single alteration.

We reported it to the committee of five. . . . I do not remember that Franklin or Sherman criticized any thing. We were all in haste. Congress was impatient, and the instrument was reported. . . . Congress cut off about a quarter of it, as I expected they would; but they obliterated some of the best of it. . . . I have long wondered that the original [draft] has not been published. I suppose the reason is the vehement **philippic**[4] against Negro slavery.

As you justly observe, there is not an idea in it but what had been **hackneyed**[5] in Congress for two years before. The substance of it is contained in the declaration of rights and the violations of those rights, in the journals of Congress, in 1774. . . .

---

[2] **conned**—studied.

[3] **courtiers**—attendants at a sovereign's court.

[4] **philippic**—bitter attack.

[5] **hackneyed**—made overfamiliar; made trite.

QUESTIONS TO CONSIDER

1. Why does John Adams refuse to write the Declaration?

2. What can you infer about Thomas Jefferson's attitude toward slavery? What can you infer about Adams's attitude toward slavery?

3. Why does Adams object to Jefferson having called King George a "tyrant"?

Fighting the
Revolutionary War

part three

The News of Washington Crossing the Delaware

BY AN OFFICER WHO WAS THERE

*The early months of the war were humiliating for the Revolutionary Army. Many Patriots had been killed, wounded, or captured, or had deserted. Many others planned on going home when their terms of duty expired on December 31, 1776. General Washington needed a victory. Always brave, sometimes to the point of recklessness, he set out on Christmas night, in the middle of a terrific snowstorm, to cross the Delaware River and attack a British **garrison**[1] at Trenton, New Jersey. The result was just as he wished, and many of his troops, now reinvigorated by victory, signed up for another tour of duty. The following is an officer's account, published by the Continental Congress only days after the crossing.*

---

[1] **garrison**—military post.

BALTIMORE, December 30. Congress received the following Intelligence from the Council of Safety, as coming from "an Officer of distinction in the Army."

Headquarters, Newtown, Bucks County. Dec. 27.

It was determined some days ago, that our army should pass over to Jersey at three different places and attack the enemy. Accordingly, about 2,500 men and 20 brass field pieces,[2] with his Excellency General Washington at their head, and Major General Sullivan and General Green in command of two divisions, passed over on the night of Christmas, and about three o'clock A.M. were on their march by two routes towards Trenton.—The night was sleety and cold, and the roads slippery, [so] that it was day break when we were two miles from Trenton, but happily the enemy were not **apprised**[3] of our design, and our advance party were on their guards at half a mile from town where General Sullivan and General Green's divisions soon came into the same road.

Their guard gave our advance party several smart fires as we drove them, but we soon got two field pieces at play and several others in a small time, and one of our columns pushing down on the right while the other advanced on the left into town. The enemy consisting of about 1500 Hessians[4] under Col. Rohl formed and made some smart fires from their musketry[5] and 6 field pieces, but our people pressed from every quarter and drove them from their cannon.—They retired towards a field behind a piece of woods up the

---

[2] field pieces—cannons.

[3] **apprised**—informed.

[4] Hessians—professional soldiers from Germany who served in the British army in America.

[5] musketry—shoulder guns.

creek from Trenton and formed two bodies, which I expected would have brought on a smart action from our troops who had formed very near them, but at that instant as I came in full view of them from the back of the woods with his Excellency General Washington, an officer informed him that one party had grounded their arms and surrendered [as our] prisoners.—The other soon followed their example, except a part which had got off in the hazy weather towards Princeton; their light horse made off on our first approach.—Too much praise cannot be given to the officers and men of every regiment, who seemed to vie with each other, and by their active spirited behavior, they soon put an honorable issue to this glorious day.

You may rejoice and be exceeding glad at this intelligence of our success, which I hope and believe will prevent the enemy from passing the river.

We took three standards, 6 fine brass cannon, and near 1000 stand of arms. They must have had about 20 or 30 killed.

I was immediately sent off with the prisoners to McConkey's ferry, and have got about seven hundred and fifty safe in town and a few miles from here, on this side [of] the ferry, viz: one Lieutenant Colonel, two Majors, four Captains, seven Lieutenants, and eight Ensigns. We left Col. Rohl, the Commandant, wounded, on his parole, and several other officers and wounded men at Trenton. We lost but two of our brave men that I can hear of, a few wounded, and one brave officer, Capt. Washington, who assisted in securing their artillery, shot in both hands. Indeed every officer and private behaved well, and it was a fortunate day to our arms, which I the more rejoice at, having an active part in it. The success of this day will greatly animate our friends, and add fresh courage to our new army, which, when formed, will be sufficient to secure us from the **depredations**[6] or insults of our enemy.

General Ewing's division could not pass at Trenton for the ice, which also impeded Gen. Cadwaladder passing over with all his cannon and the militia, though part of his troops were over, and if the whole could have passed, we should have swept the coast to Philadelphia.

Published by order of Congress.

CHARLES THOMSON, Sec'ry.

---

[6] **depredations**—plundering.

QUESTIONS TO CONSIDER

1. Why is General Washington's victory in Trenton so significant?

2. From this report, what can you infer about Washington's personality?

Washington Urges Troops to Stay Another Month

BY SERGEANT R.

After the successful attack on the British garrison at Trenton, the army learned that Lord Cornwallis, one of Britain's best generals, was marching toward them. Even the joy of victory could not overcome such problems as vile weather, lack of shoes and warm clothing, and horses that slipped and slid on the ice. Many soldiers were looking forward to going home when their terms of duty were up in a matter of days. Washington rose to the occasion, displaying his leadership ability, and his troops displayed their loyalty to him—many agreed to stay on. Here is the story, told by a noncommissioned officer known only as Sergeant R.

While we were at Trenton, on the last of December, 1776, the time for which I and most of my regiment had enlisted expired. At this trying time General Washington, having now but a little handful of men, and many of them new recruits in which he could place little confidence, ordered our regiment to be paraded, and personally addressed us, urging that we should stay a month longer. He alluded to our recent victory at Trenton, told us that our services were greatly needed, and that we could now do more for our country than we ever could at any future period, and in the most affectionate manner **entreated**[1] us to stay. The drums beat for volunteers, but not a man turned out. The soldiers, worn down by fatigue and **privations,**[2] had their hearts fixed on home and the comforts of the domestic circle, and it was hard to forgo the anticipated pleasures of the society of our dearest friends.

The General wheeled his horse about, rode in front of the regiment, and addressing us again said, "My brave fellows, you have done all I asked you to do, and more than could reasonably be expected; but your country is at stake, your wives, your houses, and all that you hold dear. You have worn yourselves out with fatigues and hardships, but we know not how to spare you. If you will consent to stay only one month longer, you will render that service to the cause of liberty, and to your country, which you probably never can do under any other circumstances. The present is emphatically the crisis, which is to decide our destiny."

The drums beat a second time. The soldiers felt the force of the appeal. One said to another, "I will remain if you will." Others remarked, "We cannot go home under such circumstances." A few stepped forth, and their

---

[1] **entreated**—pleaded; begged.

[2] **privations**—lack of the basic necessities or comforts of life.

example was immediately followed by nearly all who were fit for duty in the regiment, amounting to about two hundred volunteers. An officer inquired of the General if these men should be enrolled. He replied, "No! Men who will volunteer in such a case as this need no enrollment to keep them to their duty."

QUESTIONS TO CONSIDER

1. To what emotions or ideals in the soldiers does General Washington appeal to get them to volunteer?

2. Reread the final sentence. What is the significance of Washington declining to "enroll" the men?

The Crisis
(Number 1)

BY THOMAS PAINE

Thomas Paine was born in England in 1737 and came to America in 1774. A newcomer to the scene, he became editor of the Pennsylvania Magazine *and joined the rebel cause. His most famous work,* Common Sense, *sold 50,000 copies—a very impressive number, even by today's standards. His* Crisis *papers, published between 1776 and 1783, further served to inspire the revolutionary cause. This, the first one, was written in mid-December, 1776, just when Washington was desperate for a victory and his troops were on the verge of collapse. When Washington read it, he found it so energizing that he ordered all his troops to read it too.*

These are the times that try men's souls. The summer soldier and the sunshine patriot will, in this crisis, shrink from the service of his country; but he that stands it NOW, deserves the love and thanks of man and woman. Tyranny, like hell, is not easily conquered; yet we have this consolation with us, that the harder the conflict, the more glorious the triumph. What we obtain too cheap, we esteem too lightly: 'Tis dearness only that gives every thing its value. Heaven knows how to put a proper price upon its goods; and it would be strange indeed, if so celestial an article as FREEDOM should not be highly rated. Britain, with an army to enforce her tyranny, has declared that she has a right (*not only to* TAX) but "*to* BIND *us in* ALL CASES WHATSO-EVER," and if being *bound in that manner*, is not slavery, then is there not such a thing as slavery upon earth. Even the expression is **impious**,[1] for so unlimited a power can belong only to GOD. . . .

I have as little superstition in me as any man living, but my secret opinion has ever been, and still is, that God Almighty will not give up a people to military destruction, or leave them unsupportedly to perish, who had so earnestly and so repeatedly sought to avoid the calamities of war, by every decent method which wisdom could invent. Neither have I so much of the **infidel**[2] in me, as to suppose that HE has relinquished the government of the world, and given us up to the care of devils; and as I do not, I cannot see on what grounds the king of Britain can look up to Heaven for help against us: A common murderer, a highwayman, or a house-breaker has a good a pretence as he. . . .

I shall not now attempt to give all the particulars of our retreat to the Delaware; suffice it for the present to say, that both officers and men, though greatly harassed and fatigued, frequently without rest, covering, or pro-vision, the inevitable consequences of a long retreat, bore it with a manly and a martial spirit. All their wishes were one, which was, that the country would turn out and help them to drive the enemy back. Voltaire[3] has

---

[1] **impious**—lacking due respect.

[2] **infidel**—non-believer.

[3] Voltaire—Francois Marie Arouet Voltaire (1694–1778) was a famous writer and an influential figure during the French Enlightenment.

remarked that King William[4] never appeared to full advantage but in difficulties and in action; the same remark may be made on George Washington, for the character fits him. There is a natural firmness in some minds which cannot be unlocked by trifles, but which, when unlocked, discovers a cabinet of fortitude; and I reckon it among those kind of public blessings, which we do not immediately see, that GOD hath blest him with uninterrupted health, and given him a mind that can even flourish upon care.

I shall conclude this paper with some miscellaneous remarks on the state of our affairs; and shall begin with asking the following question, Why is it that the enemy have left the New-England provinces, and made these middle ones the seat of war? The answer is easy: New-England is not infested with tories, and we are. I have been tender in raising the cry against these men, and used numberless arguments to show them their danger, but it will not do to sacrifice a world to either their folly or their baseness. The period is now arrived, in which either they or we must change our sentiments, or one or both must fall. And what is a tory? Good GOD! what is he? I should not be afraid to go with an hundred whigs[5] against a thousand tories,[6] were they to attempt to get into arms. Every tory is a coward, for a servile, slavish, self-interested fear is the foundation of toryism; and a man under such influence, though he may be cruel, never can be brave.

But, before the line of irrecoverable separation be drawn between us, let us reason the matter together: Your conduct is an invitation to the enemy, yet not one

---

[4] King William—William III (1650–1702) was prince of Orange and later king of England, Scotland, and Ireland. He spent most of his reign resisting the expansionist plans of a powerful French monarchy.

[5] whigs—supporters of the war against England during the American Revolution. Often spelled with a captial W.

[6] tories—Americans who, during the American Revolution, favored the British side. Often spelled with a captial T. Also called Loyalists.

in a thousand of you has heart enough to join him. [General William] Howe is as much deceived by you as the American cause is injured by you. He expects you will all take up arms, and flock to his standard with muskets on your shoulders. Your opinions are of no use to him, unless you support him personally, for 'tis soldiers, and not tories, that he wants.

I once felt all that kind of anger, which a man ought to feel, against the mean principles that are held by the tories: A noted one, who kept a tavern at Amboy, was standing at his door, with as pretty a child in his hand, about eight or nine years old, as most I ever saw, and after speaking his mind as freely as he thought was prudent, finished with this unfatherly expression, *"Well! give me peace in my day."* Not a man lives on the continent but fully believes that a separation must some time or other finally take place, and a generous parent should have said, *"If there must be trouble, let it be in my day that my child may have peace"* and this single reflection, well applied, is sufficient to awaken every man to duty. Not a place upon earth might be so happy as America. Her situation is remote from all the wrangling world, and she has nothing to do but to trade with them. A man may easily distinguish in himself between temper and principle, and I am as confident, as I am that GOD governs the world, that America will never be happy till she gets clear of foreign **dominion.**[7] Wars, without ceasing, will break out till that period arrives, and the continent must in the end be conqueror; for though the flame of liberty may sometimes cease to shine, the coal never can expire. . . .

Not all the treasures of the world, so far as I believe, could have induced me to support an offensive war, for I think it murder; but if a thief break into my house, burn and destroy my property, and kill or threaten to

---

[7] **dominion**—control over an area; sovereignty.

kill me, or those that are in it, and to *"bind me in all cases whatsoever,"* to his absolute will, am I to suffer it? What signifies it to me, whether he who does it, is a king or a common man; my countryman or not my countryman? whether it is done by an individual villain, or an army of them? If we reason to the root of things we shall find no difference; neither can any just cause be assigned why we should punish in the one case and pardon in the other. Let them call me rebel, and welcome. I feel no concern from it; but I should suffer the misery of devils, were I to make a whore of my soul by swearing allegiance to one whose character is that of a sottish, stupid, stubborn, worthless, brutish man. I conceive likewise a horrid idea in receiving mercy from a being, who at the last day shall be shrieking to the rocks and mountains to cover him, and fleeing with terror from the orphan, the widow, and the slain of America.

There are cases which cannot be overdone by language, and this is one. There are persons too who see not the full extent of the evil which threatens them, they solace themselves with hopes that the enemy, if they succeed, will be merciful. It is the madness of folly to expect mercy from those who have refused to do justice; and even mercy, where conquest is the object, is only a trick of war: The cunning of the fox is as murderous as the violence of the wolf; and we ought to guard equally against both. Howe's first object is partly by threats and partly by promise, to terrify or seduce the people to deliver up their arms, and receive mercy. The ministry recommended the same plan to [General Thomas] Gage, and this is what the tories call making their peace: *"a peace which passeth all understanding"* indeed! A peace which would be the immediate forerunner of a worse ruin than any we have yet thought of. Ye men of Pennsylvania, do reason upon these things! Were the back counties to give up their arms, they would fall an easy prey to the Indians, who are all alarmed. This perhaps is what some tories would not be sorry for. Were the home counties to deliver up their arms, they would be exposed to the resentment of the back counties, who would then have it in their power to chastise their defection at pleasure. And were any one state to give up its arms, THAT state must be garrisoned by all Howe's army of Britons and Hessians to preserve it from the anger of the rest. Mutual fear is a principal link in the chain of mutual love, and woe be to that state that breaks the compact. Howe is mercifully inviting you to barbarous destruction, and men must be either rogues or fools that will not see it. I dwell not upon the powers of imagination; I bring reason to your ears; and in language as plain as A, B, C, hold up truth to your eyes.

I thank GOD that I fear not. I see no real cause for fear. I know our situation well, and can see the way out of it. While our army was collected, Howe dared not risk a battle, and it is no credit to him that he decamped from the White Plains, and waited a mean opportunity to ravage the defenceless Jerseys; but it is great credit to us, that, with a handful of men, we sustained an orderly retreat for near an hundred miles, brought off our ammunition, all our field-pieces, the greatest part of our stores, and had four rivers to pass. None can say that our retreat was **precipitate,**[8] for we were near three weeks in performing it, that the country might have time to come in. Twice we marched back to meet the enemy and remained out till dark. The sign of fear was not seen in our camp, and had not some of the cowardly and disaffected inhabitants spread false alarms through the country, the Jerseys had never been ravaged. Once more we are again collected and collecting; our new army at both ends of the continent is recruiting fast, and we shall be able to open the next campaign with sixty thousand men, well armed and clothed. This is our

---

[8] **precipitate**—hasty.

situation, and who will may know it. By perseverance and fortitude we have the prospect of a glorious issue; by cowardice and submission, the sad choice of a variety of evils—a ravaged country—a depopulated city—habitations without safety, and slavery without hope—our homes turned into barracks and **bawdy-houses**[9] for Hessians, and a future race to provide for whose fathers we shall doubt of. Look on this picture and weep over it! and if there yet remains one thoughtless wretch who believes it not, let him suffer it unlamented.

---

[9] **bawdy-houses**—brothels.

QUESTIONS TO CONSIDER

1. What are a "summer soldier" and a "sunshine patriot"?

2. What is Paine's attitude toward the Tories?

3. Why is Paine so offended by the father's words: "Well! give me peace in my day."

4. Explain in your own words Paine's powerful metaphor: "...for though the flame of liberty may sometimes cease to shine, the coal never can expire."

Songs of the Revolution

These five songs reveal the spirit of the defiant Patriots. The songs poke fun at the British, take pride in the rebellion, and tell the stories of heroic battles.

In May 1775, the "junto"[1] of British Generals William Howe, Henry Clinton, and John Burgoyne arrived at the Port of Boston to put down the rebellion. "A Junto Song" expresses the colonists' deep contempt for the generals' power and their laws. "Fish and Tea" is a protest of the taxes in the Coercive Acts of 1774 and Newfoundland Fisheries Act of March 1775. "Yankee Doodle," the most famous song in American history, is a song of praise for the New England militia. For a while it was popular with the British because they saw it as mocking Yankee cowardice. After the Battle of Bunker Hill, however, it became the marching song of the Patriot troops. "The British Lamentation," written about 1776 or 1777, was probably based on a true incident. An effective piece of propaganda, it both shows sympathy for the British soldiers who die far from home and portrays the Americans as heroes who are not afraid to die in the struggle for liberty. Finally, "Paul Jones's Victory" tells the story of the famous battle between the American commander John Paul Jones and the British sea captain Richard Pearson.

---

[1] junto—a variation of "junta." In this context it means a small group of military officers who rule after seizing power by force.

A Junto Song

'Tis money makes the member vote
        And **sanctifies**[2] our ways;
It makes the patriot turn his coat.
        And money we must raise.

        And a-taxing we will go, we'll go,
        And a-taxing we will go.

More taxes we must sure impose,
        To raise the civil list;
Also pay our ayes and noes,
        And make opposers hist.[3]

        And a-taxing we will go, etc.

One single thing untaxed at home,
        Old England could not show,
For money we abroad did roam,
        And thought to tax the new.

        And a-taxing we will go, etc.

The power supreme of Parliament,
        Our purpose did assist,
And taxing laws abroad were sent,
        Which rebels do resist.

        And a-taxing we will go, etc.

---

[2] **sanctifie**s—makes holy or spiritual.

[3] hist—short for "history."

Shall we not make the rascals bend
        To Britain's supreme power?
The sword shall we not to them send,
        And leaden balls a shower?

    And a-taxing we will go, etc.

Boston we shall in ashes lay,
        It is a nest of **knaves:**[4]
We'll make them soon for mercy pray,
        Or send them to their graves.

    And a-taxing we will go, etc.

But second thoughts are ever best,
        And lest our force should fail,
What fraud can do, we'll make a test,
        And see what bribes avail.

    And a-taxing we will go, etc.

Each colony, we will propose,
        Shall raise an ample sum;
Which well applied, under the rose,
        May bribe them—as at home.

    And a-taxing we will go, etc.

We'll force and fraud in one unite,
        To bring them to our hands;
Then lay a tax on the sun's light,
        And king's tax on their lands.

    And a-taxing we will go, etc.

---

[4] **knaves**—unprincipled, crafty men.

Fish and Tea

What a court hath old England of folly and sin,
Spite of Chatham and Camden, Barre, Burke, Wilkes
 and Glynn![5]
Not content with the game act, they tax fish and sea,
And America drench with hot water and tea.

> *Derry down, down, down derry down.*

But if the wise Council of England doth think,
They may be enslaved by the power of drink,
They're right to enforce it; but then, do you see?
The Colonies, too, may refuse and be free.

> *Derry down, down, down derry down.*

There's no knowing where this oppression will stop;
Some say—there's no cure but a capital chop;
And that I believe's each American's wish,
Since you've drenched 'em with tea, and depriv'd
 'em of fish.

> *Derry down, down, down derry down.*

The birds of the air, and the fish of the sea,
By the gods, for poor Dan Adam's use were made free,
Till a man with more power, than old Moses would wish,
Said, "Ye wretches, ye shan't touch a fowl or a fish!"

> *Derry down, down, down derry down.*

---

[5] Members of Parliament who had spoken in support of the colonists and against the taxes. They are William Pitt, the Earl of Chatham; Lord Camden, the Chief Justice of the Court of Common Pleas; Colonel Isaac Barre; satirist Edmund Burke; and journalist John Wilkes.

Three Generals these mandates have borne 'cross the sea,
To deprive 'em of fish and to make 'em drink tea;
In turn, sure, these freemen will boldly agree,
To give 'em a dance upon Liberty Tree.

Derry down, down, down derry down.

Then *freedom's* the word, both at home and abroad,
And [away] every scabbard that hides a good sword!
Our forefathers gave us this freedom in hand,
And we'll die in defence of the rights of the land.

Derry down, down, down derry down.

Yankee Doodle

Father and I went down to camp,
    Along with Captain Gooding,
There we see the men and boys
    As thick as hasty pudding.

Yankee[6] doodle, keep it up,
        Yankee doodle, dandy;
Mind the music and the step,
        And with the girls be handy.

And there we see a thousand men,
    As rich as Squire David;
And what they wasted every day,
    I wish it could be saved.

---

[6] Yankee—a New Englander. The British were responsible for the term being applied to anyone from the United States.

Yankee doodle, etc.

The 'lasses they eat every day,
   Would keep an house a winter;
They have as much that I'll be bound
   They eat it when they're amind to.

Yankee doodle, etc.

And there we see a swamping gun,
   Large as a log of maple,
Upon a deuced little cart,
   A load for father's cattle.

Yankee doodle, etc.

And every time they shoot it off,
   It takes a horn of powder;
It makes a noise like father's gun,
   Only a nation louder.

Yankee doodle, etc.

I went as **nigh**[7] to one myself,
   As 'Siah's **underpinning;**[8]
And father went as nigh again,
   I thought the deuce was in him.

Yankee doodle, etc.

Cousin Simon grew so bold,
   I thought he would have cock'd it:
It scar'd me so, I shrink'd it off,
   And hung by father's pocket.

---

[7] **nigh**—near.

[8] **underpinning**—legs.

Yankee doodle, etc.

And Captain Davis had a gun,
   He kind of clap'd his hand on't,
And struck a crooked stabbing iron
   Upon the little end on't.

Yankee doodle, etc.

And there I see a pumpkin shell
   As big as mother's basin,
And every time they touch'd it off,
   They scamper'd like the nation.

Yankee doodle, etc.

I see a little barrel too,
   The heads were made of leather,
They knock'd upon't with little clubs,
   And call'd the folks together.

Yankee doodle, etc.

And there was Captain Washington,
   And gentlefolks about him,
They say he's grown so tarnal[9] proud,
   He will not ride without 'em.

Yankee doodle, etc.

---

[9] tarnal—darned.

He got him on his meeting clothes,
    Upon a slapping stallion,
He set the world along in rows,
    In hundreds and in millions.

       Yankee doodle, etc.

The flaming ribbons in their hats,
    They look'd so taring fine, ah,
I wanted pockily to get,
    To give to my Jemimah.

       Yankee doodle, etc.

I see another snarl of men
    A-digging graves, they told me,
So tarnal long, so tarnal deep,
    They 'tended they should hold me.

       Yankee doodle, etc.

It scar'd me so, I hook'd it off,
    Nor stopt, as I remember,
Nor turn'd about till I got home,
    Lock'd up in mother's chamber.

       Yankee doodle, etc.

The British Lamentation

Come all you good people, wherever you be.
Who walk on the land or sail by the sea;
Come listen to the words of a dying man,
I think that you'll remember them.
'Twas on December the sixteenth day
That we set sail for America;
Our drums did beat and trumpets sound
And unto Boston we were bound.
And when to Boston we did come
We thought by the aid of our British guns
To drive the rebels from that place
And fill their hearts with sore disgrace.

But to our sad and sore surprise,
We saw men like grasshoppers rise:
They fought like heroes much enraged
Which surely frightened General Gage.

Like lions roaring for their prey
They feared no danger nor dismay;
True British blood runs through their veins
And them with courage yet sustains.

We saw those bold Columbia sons,
Spread death and slaughter from their guns,
Freedom or death! was all their cry,
They did not seem to fear to die.

We sailed to York, as you've been told
With the loss of many a Briton bold,
For to make those rebels own our King,
And daily tribute to him bring.

They said it was a garden place,
And that our armies could, with ease,
Pull down their towns; lay waste their lands,
In spite of all their boasted bands.

A garden place it was indeed,
And in it grew many a bitter weed,
Which did pull down our highest hopes
And sorely wound the British troops.
'Tis now September the seventeenth day,
I wish I'd ne'er come to America,
Full fifteen hundred has been slain
Bold British heroes every one.

Now I've received my deathly wound,
I bid farewell to England's ground;
My wife and children will mourn for me,
Whilst I lie cold in America.

Fight on, America's noble sons,
Fear not Brittania's thundering guns,
Maintain your rights from year to year,
God's on your side, you need not fear.

Paul Jones's Victory

An American **frigate,**[10] a frigate of fame,
With guns mounted forty, the *Richard*[11] by name,
For to cruise in the channel of old England,
And a valiant commander,
Paul Jones is the man.

We had not sailed long before we did spy
A large forty-four, and a twenty so nigh,
With fifty bold seamen well laid in with store,
In consort pursued us from the old English shore.
About twelve at noon Pearson came alongside,
With a speaking trumpet; "Whence came you?" he cried,
"It's now give an answer, I hail'd you before,
Or this moment a broadside into you I will pour."

Paul Jones then he says to his men every one,
"Let every bold seaman stand true to his gun;
We'll receive a broadside from these bold Englishmen,
And like true Yankee heroes return it again."

The contest was bloody, both decks ran with gore,
The sea seemed to blaze when the cannon did roar;
"Fight on my brave boys," then Paul Jones he cried,
"We will soon humble this bold Englishman's pride."

We fought them eight glasses, eight glasses so hot,
Till seventy bold seamen lay dead on the spot,
And ninety bold seamen lay bleeding in gore,
While the pieces of cannon like thunder did roar.

---

[10] **frigate**—a high-speed, medium-sized sailing war vessel of the 17th, 18th, and 19th centuries.

[11] The battle, fought on the night of September 23, 1779, included several ships. Jones commanded a squadron including the *Bonhomme Richard, Pallas, Alliance,* and *Vengeance.* In Pearson's fleet were the 50-gun *Serapis* and the 20-gun *Countess of Scarborough.* John Paul Jones was the victor, but the *Bonhomme Richard* was so battle damaged that she sank two days later.

Our gunner in a fright to Paul Jones he came;
"We make water quite fast, and our side's in a flame";
Then brave Jones he said in the height of his pride,
"If we can't do no better boys, sink alongside."
The Alliance bore down while the Richard did rake,
Which caused the heart of poor Pearson to ache;
Our shot flew so hot they could not stand us long,
And the flag of proud Britain was forced to come down.

So now my brave boys, you have taken a prize,
A large forty-four and a twenty likewise,
Both noble vessels well laden with store,
We'll bend on all canvas for New England once more.
God bless the widows who shortly must weep
For the loss of their husbands now sunk in the deep;
Here's a health to Paul Jones, a sword in his hand,
Who led us to battle and gave the command!

QUESTIONS TO CONSIDER

1. In "A Junto Song" and "Fish and Tea," what motivates
   the British?

2. What in the song might have led the British to think that
   "Yankee Doodle" was meant to poke fun at the Patriots?

3. Which lines in "The British Lamentation" seem like
   propaganda?

4. What types of emotions might the ballad "Paul Jones's
   Victory" have inspired in the Patriots?

A Hessian General's Wife Describes the Horrors of Battle

BY BARONESS VON RIEDESEL

General Baron von Riedesel was a professional soldier from the German region of Hesse. He belonged to a large mercenary force hired by the British to assist in putting down the Revolution. The Baron was fighting in General Burgoyne's army. He was accompanied by his wife and children. His wife, the Baroness, kept a journal throughout the war that provides a close-up picture of the misery that was their life day in and day out.

Toward evening [of October 9, 1777], we at last came to Saratoga, which was only half an hour's march from the place where we had spent the whole day. I was wet through and through by the frequent rains, and was obliged to remain in this condition the entire night, as I had no place whatever where I could change my linen. I, therefore, seated myself before a good fire, and undressed my children; after which, we laid ourselves down together upon some straw. I asked General Phillips, who came up to where we were, why we did not continue our retreat while there was yet time, as my husband had pledged himself to cover it and bring the army through.

"Poor woman," answered he, "I am amazed at you! completely wet through, have you still the courage to wish to go further in this weather! Would that you were only our commanding general! He halts because he is tired, and intends to spend the night here and give us a supper."

In this latter achievement, especially, General Burgoyne was very fond of indulging. He spent half the nights in singing and drinking, and amusing himself with the wife of a commissary, who was his mistress, and who, as well as he, loved champagne.

On the 10th, at seven o'clock in the morning, I drank some tea by way of refreshment; and we now hoped from one moment to another that at last we would again get under way. General Burgoyne, in order to cover our retreat, caused the beautiful houses and mills at Saratoga, belonging to General Schuyler, to be burned. An English officer brought some excellent broth, which he shared with me, as I was not able to refuse his urgent entreaties.

Whereupon we set out upon our march, but only as far as another place not far from where we had started. The greatest misery and the utmost disorder prevailed in the army. The commissaries had forgotten to distribute provisions among the troops. There were cattle enough, but not one had been killed. More than thirty officers came to me, who could endure hunger no longer. I had coffee and tea made for them, and divided among them all the provisions with which my carriage was constantly filled; for we had a cook who, although an arrant knave,[1] was fruitful in all expedients, and often in the night crossed small rivers in order to steal from the country people sheep, poultry and pigs. . . .

The whole army clamored for a retreat, and my husband promised to make it possible, provided only that no time was lost. But General Burgoyne, to whom an order had been promised if he brought about a junction with the army of General Howe, could not determine upon this course, and lost every thing by his loitering.

About two o'clock in the afternoon, the firing of cannon and small arms was again heard, and all was alarm and confusion. My husband sent me a message telling me to betake myself forthwith into a house which was not far from there. I seated myself in the calash[2] with my children, and had scarcely driven up to the house when I saw on the opposite side of the Hudson River five or six men with guns, which were aimed at us. Almost involuntarily I threw the children on the bottom of the calash and myself over them. At the same instant the **churls**[3] fired, and shattered the arm of a poor English soldier behind us, who was already wounded, and was also on the point of retreating into the house.

Immediately after our arrival a frightful cannonade began, principally directed against the house in which we had sought shelter, probably because the enemy believed, from seeing so many people flocking around it, that all the generals made it their headquarters. Alas! it harbored none but wounded soldiers, or women! We were finally obliged to take refuge in a cellar, in which I laid myself down in a corner not far from the door. My children lay down on the earth with their heads upon my lap, and in this manner we passed the entire night. A horrible stench, the cries of the children, and yet more than all this, my own anguish, prevented me from

---

[1] arrant knave—dishonest rascal.

[2] calash—light, low carriage with a folding top.

[3] **churls**—rude, boorish people.

closing my eyes. On the following morning the cannon-ade again began, but from a different side. I advised all to go out of the cellar for a little while, during which time I would have it cleaned, as otherwise we would all be sick. They followed my suggestion, and I at once set many hands to work, which was in the highest degree necessary; for the women and children, being afraid to venture forth, had soiled the whole cellar.

After they had all gone out and left me alone, I for the first time surveyed our place of refuge. It consisted of three beautiful cellars, splendidly arched. I proposed that the most dangerously wounded of the officers should be brought into one of them; that the women should remain in another; and that all the rest should stay in the third, which was nearest the entrance. I had just given the cellars a good sweeping, and had fumi-gated them by sprinkling vinegar on burning coals, and each one had found his place prepared for him—when a fresh and terrible cannonade threw us all once more into alarm. Many persons, who had no right to come in, threw themselves against the door. My children were already under the cellar steps, and we would all have been crushed, if God had not given me strength to place myself before the door, and with extended arms prevent all from coming in; otherwise every one of us would have been severely injured.

Eleven cannon balls went through the house, and we could plainly hear them rolling over our heads. One poor soldier, whose leg they were about to amputate, having been laid upon a table for this purpose, had the other leg taken off by another cannon ball, in the very middle of the operation. His comrades all ran off, and when they again came back they found him in one corner of the room, where he had rolled in his anguish, scarcely breathing. I was more dead than alive, though not so much on account of our own danger as for that which enveloped my husband, who, however, frequently sent to see how I was getting along, and to tell me that he was still safe. . . .

Our cook saw to our meals, but we were in want of water; and in order to quench thirst, I was often obliged to drink wine and give it, also, to the children. It was, moreover, the only thing that my husband could take, which fact so worked upon our faithful Rockel that he said to me one day, "I fear that the general drinks so much wine because he dreads falling into captivity, and is therefore weary of life." The continual danger in which my husband was encompassed was a constant source of anxiety to me. I was the only one of all the women whose husband had not been killed or wounded, and I often said to myself—especially since my husband was placed in such great danger day and night—"Shall I be the only fortunate one?" He never came into the tent at night, but lay outside by the watch fires. This alone was sufficient to have caused his death, as the nights were damp and cold.

As the great scarcity of water continued, we at last found a soldier's wife who had the courage to bring water from the river, for no one else would undertake it, as the enemy shot at the head of every man who approached the river. This woman, however, they never molested; and they told us afterward that they spared her on account of her sex.

I endeavored to divert my mind from my troubles by constantly busying myself with the wounded. I made them tea and coffee, and received in return a thousand **benedictions.**[4] Often, also, I shared my noonday meal with them. One day a Canadian officer came into our cellar who could scarcely stand up. We at last got it out of him that he was almost dead with hunger. I considered myself very fortunate to have it in my power to offer

---

[4] **benedictions**—blessings.

him my mess. This gave him renewed strength, and gained for me his friendship. . . .

In this horrible situation we remained six days. Finally, they spoke of **capitulating**,[5] as by **temporizing**[6] for so long a time our retreat had been cut off. A cessation of hostilities took place, and my husband, who was thoroughly worn out, was able, for the first time in a long while, to lie down upon a bed. In order that his rest might not be in the least disturbed, I had a good bed made up for him in a little room; while I, with my children and both my maids, lay down in a little parlor close by. But about one o'clock in the night someone came and asked to speak to him. It was with the greatest reluctance that I found myself obliged to awaken him. I observed that the message did not please him, as he immediately sent the man back to headquarters and laid himself down again considerably out of humor.

Soon after this General Burgoyne requested the presence of all the generals and staff officers at a council of war, which was to be held early the next morning; in which he proposed to break the capitulation, already made with the enemy, in consequence of some false information just received. It was, however, finally decided that this was neither practicable nor advisable; and this was fortunate for us, as the Americans said to us afterwards that had the capitulation been broken we all would have been massacred; which they could have done the more easily as we were not over four or five thousand men strong, and had given them time to bring together more than twenty thousand. . . .

At last my husband sent to me a groom with a message that I should come to him with our children. I, therefore, again seated myself in my dear calash; and in the passage through the American camp I observed with

[5] **capitulating**—negotiating.
[6] **temporizing**—delaying.

great satisfaction that no one cast at us scornful glances. On the contrary, they all greeted me, even showing compassion on their countenances at seeing a mother with her little children in such a situation. I confess that I feared to come into the enemy's camp, as the thing was so entirely new to me.

When I approached the tents, a noble-looking man came toward me, took the children out of the wagon, embraced and kissed them, and then with tears in his eyes helped me also to alight. "You tremble," said he to me. "Fear nothing."

"No," replied I, "for you are so kind, and have been so tender toward my children, that it has inspired me with courage."

He then led me to the tent of General Gates, with whom I found Generals Burgoyne and Phillips, who were upon an extremely friendly footing with him.

Burgoyne said to me, "You may now dismiss all your apprehensions, for your sufferings are at an end."

I answered him that I should certainly be acting very wrongly to have any more anxiety when our chief had none, and especially when I saw him on such friendly footing with General Gates. All the generals remained to dine with General Gates.

The man who had received me so kindly came up and said to me, "It may be embarrassing to you to dine with all these gentlemen; come now with your children into my tent, where I will give you, it is true, a frugal meal, but one that will be accompanied by the best of wishes."

"You are certainly," answered I, "a husband and a father, since you show me so much kindness."

I then learned that he was the American General Schuyler. He entertained me with excellent smoked tongue, beefsteaks, potatoes, good butter and bread.

Never have I eaten a better meal. I was content. I saw that all around me were so likewise; but that which rejoiced me more than everything else was that my husband was out of all danger. As soon as we had finished dinner, he invited me to take up my residence at his house, which was situated in Albany, and told me that General Burgoyne would, also, be there. I sent and asked my husband what I should do. He sent me word to accept the invitation; and as it was two days' journey from where we were, and already five o'clock in the afternoon, he advised me to set out in advance, and to stay over night at a place distant about three hours' ride. General Schuyler was so obliging as to send with me a French officer, who was a very agreeable man and commanded those troops who composed the reconnoitering party of which I have before made mention. As soon as he had escorted me to the house where we were to remain, he went back. . . .

The day after this we arrived at Albany, where we had so often longed to be. But we came not, as we supposed we should, as victors! We were, nevertheless, received in the most friendly manner by the good General Schuyler, and by his wife and daughters, who showed us the most marked courtesy, as, also, General Burgoyne, although he had—without any necessity it was said—caused their magnificently built houses to be burned. But they treated us as people who knew how to forget their own losses in the misfortunes of others.

Even General Burgoyne was deeply moved at their magnanimity and said to General Schuyler, "Is it to me, who have done you so much injury, that you show so much kindness!"

"That is the fate of war," replied the brave man; "let us say no more about it."

We remained three days with them, and they acted as if they were very reluctant to let us go.

QUESTIONS TO CONSIDER

1. What are some of Baroness von Riedesel's duties?

2. What opinion does the Baroness have of General Burgoyne? Why is this her opinion?

3. Why do you think the Revolutionary soldiers are so kind to the Hessians?

Winter at Valley Forge

BY JOHN TEBBEL

General Washington's army was camped at Valley Forge near Philadelphia during the winter of 1777–1778. The stories told of this winter have always emphasized the terrible hardships the army faced because they lacked such basic necessities as food, fresh water, warm clothes, and shoes or boots. Here journalist and historian John Tebbel explains what it was really like and why.

Private Joseph Martin remembered his first sight of Valley Forge. It was dark, there was no water, "and I was perishing with thirst. I searched for water till I was weary, and came to my tent without finding any. Fatigue and thirst, joined with hunger, almost made me desperate. I felt at that instant as if I would have taken victuals or drink from the best friend I had on earth by force."

Two soldiers passed by him with full canteens, but they wouldn't give him any and it was so dark they couldn't tell him where they got it. He begged for a swallow, offered them a threepence, all he had in the world, and got his grudging drink. "I lay there two nights and one day," he wrote later, "and had not a morsel of anything to eat all the time, save half of a small pumpkin, which I cooked by placing it upon a rock, the skin side uppermost and making a fire upon it. By the time it was heated through I devoured it with as keen an appetite as I should a pie made of it at some other time."

Martin was one of the more fortunate who didn't spend the whole winter at Valley Forge. His regiment went on to Milltown, now Downingtown, halfway between Philadelphia and Lancaster, where he became a part of a more or less permanent foraging party.[1]

In our national memory, perpetuated by artists, Valley Forge is an image of snow and bitter cold, and we think of Washington, kneeling in what looks like a snowdrift, asking God to ease the burden, something he would never have thought of doing. In fact, it's one of the mildest winters on record there, no more than two inches of snow. The enemies are rain and mud, and the chill that goes with them—these and, of course, the lack of almost everything that human beings need to live. The other enemies include hunger, disease, and the constant choking smoke of greenwood fires that make the soldiers' huts habitable. Many of these men haven't been paid for a year. Many others have not much more than a torn blanket with which to protect themselves. And there will be three periods during the winter when there's no food of any kind.

How can this be, in the heart of an agricultural country which has just produced one of its best fall harvests, war or no war? There's an abundance of beef in Connecticut, and plenty of pork in New Jersey. Boston

---

[1] foraging party—a group wandering in search of food or provisions.

warehouses are filled with cloth. New York reports surpluses of wheat, barley, and rye. So why are we starving and aching with misery in Valley Forge?

Greed and profiteering, also plain old human meanness. Even if these didn't exist, however, it's a country with such appalling roads and too few wheeled vehicles to travel them that moving supplies from one place to another is a logistical nightmare. General Mifflin, who's been serving as **quartermaster,**[2] resigns the job in November 1777, and for three months Congress doesn't appoint a successor. These, of course, are the worst months in winter quarters.

The nearest sources of supply for Valley Forge are the abundant Pennsylvania farms, but the farmers won't sell to their fellow Americans if they can get higher prices from the British in Philadelphia. William Ellery, who signed the Declaration for Rhode Island, looks about him in the Continental Congress and at the burgeoning states and writes, with disgust: "The love of country and public virtues are annihilated. If Diogenes[3] were alive and were to search America with candles, would he find an honest man?"

A colonel from New York writes to his governor, George Clinton, pleading for supplies from the stores of his home state: "I have upwards of seventy men unfit for duty only for the want of clothing, twenty of which have no breeches at all, so that they are obliged to take their blankets to cover their nakedness and as many without a single shirt, stocking, or shoe, about thirty fit for duty, the rest sick or lame, and, God knows, it won't be long before they will all be laid up, as the poor fellows are obliged to fetch wood and

---

[2] **quartermaster**—an officer responsible for the food, clothing, and equipment of troops.

[3] Diogenes—Diogenes of Sinope, who died approximately 320 B.C., was a Greek philosopher who spent his life criticizing what he thought of as a corrupt society. He is said to have roamed the streets of Athens with a lantern in hand, claiming to be searching for an honest man—but never finding one.

water on their backs half a mile with bare legs in snow or mud."

The men live in a city of log huts, twelve to a hut. Officers of the company share a hut. They're claustrophobic, these quarters, only fourteen by sixteen feet, reeking with smoke from round-the-clock fires. Before real deprivation sets in, flour or some other kind of ground grain is the primary—and sometimes the only—food. Soldiers mix water with it and bake it in pans over the coals. Fire cakes, they're called. One officer has a cherished recipe for cooking spoiled pork and hog fodder when it's available. Company-grade officers share the general misery, but the field-grade and general officers are much better supplied.

It's not a place where men sit huddled up and miserable, although they do that too. The camp is always bustling, with civilians coming and going on visits, and soldiers leaving and departing on furloughs. Nor are the food shortages common to all; some units fare better than others. Shortage of clothing is more prevalent and there are even some officers who wear blankets instead of overcoats, and apparently think nothing of standing next to men in rags. It isn't that no clothing is available, but civilians are competing for it and frequently get there first. Soldiers desperate for money are willing to break all the laws and sell what clothing they do have, even their muskets, for money to buy food and liquor. They have their own priorities. So have the civilians. Connecticut's beef supply disappears because the state puts a ceiling on the exorbitant prices farmers are getting for it, so they refuse to sell. Boston merchants have plenty of clothing on their shelves but they won't sell it, even at outrageous prices, for anything but cash. Private contractors are getting rich. They load up Pennsylvania wagons with flour and iron and send them north, while New Jersey pork rots for lack of transport. It's graft, speculation, selfishness, and incredible mismanagement everywhere, then and throughout the war.

But it's the day-to-day misery that's so awful. Lafayette, getting over his Brandywine wounds, writes home: "The unfortunate soldiers were in want of everything; they had neither coats, nor hats, nor shirts, nor shoes; their feet and legs froze till they grew black, and it was often necessary to amputate them."

A surgeon named Albigence Waldo gives us the best picture of what it's like at Valley Forge in the diary he keeps. Waldo is a remarkable man. A Pomfret, Connecticut, boy, he's grown up to be one of the best surgeons of his day and has already been a huge help in inoculating the army against **smallpox.**[4] He may be best known for his charities, which are so numerous he often doesn't have enough for his family. Waldo loves music, painting, and drawing, and on proper occasions he appears as an accomplished orator.

Waldo came to Valley Forge optimistic that maybe it wouldn't be such a bad place after all, but soon enough he's writing: "Poor food—hard lodging—cold weather—fatigue—nasty clothes—nasty cookery—vomit half my time—smoked out of my senses—the Devil's in't—I can't endure it—why are we sent here to starve and freeze—what sweet felicities have I left at home! A charming wife—pretty children—good beds—good food—good cookery—all agreeable—all harmonious. Here all confusion—smoke and cold, hunger and filthiness—a pox on my bad luck."

Waldo writes of a young soldier who comes to him nearly naked, crying out in wretchedness and despair: "I am sick, my feet lame, my legs are sore, my body covered with this tormenting itch—my clothes are worn out, my constitution is broken, my former activity is

---

[4] **smallpox**—an acute, highly infectious, often fatal disease.

exhausted by fatigue, hunger, and cold. I fail fast. I shall soon be no more! And all the reward I shall get will be, 'poor Will is dead!'"

For himself, Waldo is bitter about the people back home who "are willing we should suffer everything for their benefit and advantage, and yet are the first to condemn us for not doing more!"

If anyone's worse off, Waldo says, it's the poor Americans in Philadelphia and New York prisons, where one prisoner is so desperate from hunger that he eats his own fingers up to the first joint. Others eat clay, lime, stone chips from walls, and some who fall dead in the yard have pieces of bark, wood, or stone still in their mouths, unable to swallow them.

The cry of "No meat! No meat!" sounds dismally in the camp streets at Valley Forge, and once when a butcher does bring in a quarter of very poor beef, displaying white buttons on the knees of his breeches, a soldier cries out, "There, there, Tom, is some more of your fat beef, by my soul I can see butcher's breeches' buttons through it."

Paradoxically, Waldo believes that in some ways the officers are worse off than the soldiers. A soldier's family is provided for by public expense "if the articles they want are above the common price," but an officer's family is not so protected and has to beg for necessities, and then pay exorbitant prices for them. Officers constantly get letters of complaint from their families at home. . . . Usually the men read these when they're wet, cold, ill, or exhausted, which is much of the time.

As Waldo puts it, these missives are "filled with the most heart-breaking tender complaints a woman is capable of writing; acquainting him with the incredible difficulty with which she procures a little bread for herself and children—and finally concluding with expressions bordering on despair, of procuring a sufficiency of food to keep soul and body together through the winter—that her money is of very little consequence to her—that she begs of him to consider that charity begins at home, and not suffer his family to perish with want in the midst of plenty."

No wonder more than fifty officers of General Greene's division resign their commissions in a single day, and six or seven more the next day. Washington remarks grimly that in the end he may be left alone with the soldiers. Waldo himself, in ill health and the recipient of the same kind of letters from home that he's been writing about in his diary, resigns in October 1779.

As for the other ranks, they write home too and exchange miseries, but somehow the public doesn't really understand what's happening at Valley Forge, because Washington makes every effort to keep the desperate condition of the army a secret from the general public, which wants to hear only good news, as though he had any to give them.

QUESTIONS TO CONSIDER

1. How do the facts of the winter at Valley Forge differ from our national memory of this time?

2. Why is there a shortage of food at Valley Forge?

3. Why do army officers begin resigning in record numbers?

4. Why doesn't Washington speak out on behalf of his men?

Fighting the War

Washington Crossing the Delaware The *New York Mirror* commissioned this engraving to show its readers the Christmas night attack on the British garrison at Trenton, New Jersey.

▲

Winter at Valley Forge Baron Frederick von Steuben gave the troops strict discipline and new drilling techniques. The army came through the difficult winter ready for battle.

▲
Molly Pitcher, the Heroine of Monmouth She was called "Molly Pitcher" because she carried water back and forth from a well to the exhausted and wounded soldiers during the scorching heat of June 28, 1778. She became a heroine when she took over the cannon and continued to fire it after her gunner husband collapsed from the heat.

▲

Rebecca Motte sacrifices her new house. The British have taken over the Mottes' new mansion and sent Mrs. Motte to the old farmhouse outside the fort's walls. To drive them out, the army must set the house on fire. When the Revolutionary officers tell her, she is glad to contribute to the good of her country and offers them a fine bow and arrows to shoot flames at the roof.

Combat between Captain Pearson and John Paul Jones
An engraving by Balthasar F. Leizelt of the famous battle between Jones and Pearson. See page 122. ▶

Naval hero John Paul Jones commanded the *Bonhomme Richard.* When his ship received an especially fierce volley of shots and he was asked if he would surrender, he replied, "I have not yet begun to fight!"

▲

Benjamin Franklin Franklin's role in the war effort was as a commissioner to France. He arrived in December 1776, and became immensely popular there. His negotiations succeeded, and treaties signed in 1778 secured an important ally. By war's end, the French had sent 12,000 soldiers and 32,000 sailors to the American cause. Over 70 years old while in France, Franklin is shown in this painting as a young man of 20.

▲

Marquis de Lafayette The French aristocrat fought as a general in Washington's army. In the final days of the war, he drove Cornwallis's army across Virginia and held it in Yorktown while the other Patriot forces advanced there.

▲

The caption for this cartoon reads, *"THE HORSE* AMERICA, *throwing his Master.* Published as the Act directs. August 1, 1779 by Wm. White. Angel Court. Westminster."* The rider is King George III.

▲

Surrender of Lord Cornwallis This painting, depicting Cornwallis's surrender at Yorktown, Virginia, October 19, 1781, takes liberties with the facts. As we know from Sarah Osborn's account on page 153, Cornwallis did not show up for the ceremony.

Report of an Attack by the British and Their Indian Allies

FROM THE *NEW JERSEY JOURNAL*, APRIL 28, 1781

Most Native Americans sided with the British in the war. They viewed the colonists as the enemy who had taken their lands. The colonists, in turn, viewed the Native Americans as "savages." Stories of wartime atrocities served to support their view. Journalists played to their readers' prejudices. The following newspaper report of mayhem and bravery satisfied its audience. It is from Diary of the American Revolution. This remarkable book, first published in 1861, is historian Frank Moore's collection of newspaper reports, letters, songs, and broadsides—the large sheets of paper printed on one side and tacked up in public places that were the news channel of the 18th century.

NEW YORK Last Wednesday night a party of Indians, consisting of twenty-five, with two Tory pilots, crossed the river Delaware opposite Minisink, the principal settlement of that country. At daybreak they proceeded to the house of Thomas Brink, whom they made prisoner, with his two little sons, then plundered and destroyed every thing of any value in the house. From thence they went to the widow Brink's, distant about one hundred yards, robbed her of every valuable thing in the house, and destroyed all her provisions; then marched to a house near by, where lived two young men by the names of Westbrook and Job. They entered the house while the family were asleep; the men waked in a surprise, sprung out of bed, and made all the resistance possible, but being greatly overpowered by numbers, fell a sacrifice to savage Indians and Tories, and experienced that torture in death, which nothing but British and savage cruelty could invent. At this house they made Job's wife, and a girl about thirteen years old, prisoners. They next proceeded to Captain Shimer's, where they made three of his Negroes prisoners; six rushed into a room next to where Captain Shimer lay, while the rest surrounded the house. An old Negro woman ran to her master's bedside, and cried out, "The Indians are all around the house, and the next room is full of them." Upon which information he left his bed in a moment, seized his rifle, ran to the front door of the room, opened it, and saw about ten Indians before the piazza, when he presented his piece briskly from one to another which induced the whole to run to the rear of the house; he then, by the same stratagem, drove the whole out of his house. In the mean time, two of his Negroes got clear, whom he fixed at the two front doors of the house, each with an axe, with orders to defend them to the last extremity, then ran up to the second story, and began to fire out of the windows, when he soon got the assistance of a man who lay in one of the upper bed-rooms; they continued a brisk fire for near an hour, running from window to window, and making all the parade possible. The Indians continued a sharp fire upon the house during the whole time, but such was the unparalleled bravery and good conduct of Captain Shimer, that they despaired of effecting their cursed design, and began to retreat with their prisoners and plunder. At this moment Captain Shimer got a reinforcement of four good marksmen, when he put on his breeches and shoes (having fought all the morning in his shirt) and pursued them to the river, near a mile from his house, where he found that about one-half had crossed. He continued his pursuit with a brisk fire after the others, crying out: "Rush on, my brave boys; we'll surround them!" which so terrified the cowardly murderers, though double in number, that they ran into a swamp, leaving behind them their plunder, Mrs. Job, her little girl, and a Negro man belonging to Captain Shimer. They took Mr. Brink and his two boys over with the first party. Captain Shimer, going into a back bedroom to discharge his piece, providentially prevented his two daughters, one a young woman, the other Captain Bonnel's wife with a child in her arms, from jumping out of the window, as they were just lifting up the sash for that purpose, which was at least eighteen feet from the ground. The loss of the enemy we cannot ascertain. During the action they were seen to carry off one on a board, and several were carried away from the Pennsylvania shore; there was likewise a considerable quantity of blood seen where they passed.

QUESTIONS TO CONSIDER

1. How are the Indians and Tories portrayed in this article?

2. How is Captain Shimer portrayed?

3. What words and sentences in this newspaper article contribute to its sensational tone?

A Patriot Sergeant's Wife Tells of Life with the Army

BY SARAH OSBORN

The married soldiers often took their wives with them. In the military camps, these women performed the services that support troops perform today—preparing meals, managing supplies, washing clothes, mending clothes, and caring for the wounded. Sarah Osborn was such a wife. "Volunteered" by her commissary-sergeant husband to work alongside him for three years in a New York regiment, Sarah later filed for a war widow's pension. Here, in her deposition to a court clerk, she describes the battle of Yorktown and British surrender. She uses the word deponent *to refer to herself.*

They continued their march to Philadelphia, depo-nent on horseback through the streets, and arrived at a place toward the Schuylkill where the British had burnt some houses, where they encamped for the afternoon and night. Being out of bread, deponent was employed in baking the afternoon and evening. Deponent recollects no females but Sergeant Lamberson's and Lieutenant Forman's wives and a colored woman by the name of Letta. The Quaker ladies who came round urged deponent to stay, but her husband said, "No, he could not leave her behind." Accordingly, next day they continued their march from day to day till they arrived at Baltimore, where deponent and her said husband and the forces . . . embarked on board a vessel and sailed down the Chesapeake. There were several vessels along, and deponent was in the foremost. . . . They continued sail until they had got up the St. James River as far as the tide would carry them, about twelve miles from the mouth, and then landed, and the tide being spent, they had a fine time catching sea lobsters, which they ate.

They, however, marched immediately for a place called Williamsburg, deponent alternately on horseback and on foot. There arrived, they remained two days till the army all came in by land and then marched for Yorktown. . . . The York troops were posted at the right, the Connecticut troops next, and the French to the left. In about one day or less than a day, they reached the place of encampment about one mile from Yorktown. Deponent was on foot, and the other females above named, and her said husband still on the commissary's guard.

Deponent's attention was arrested by the appearance of a large plain between them and Yorktown and an entrenchment thrown up. She also saw a number of dead Negroes lying round their encampment, whom she understood the British had driven out of the town and left to starve, or were first starved and then thrown out. Deponent took her stand just back of the American tents, say about a mile from the town, and busied herself washing, mending, and cooking for the soldiers, in which she was assisted by the other females; some men washed their own clothing. She heard the roar of the artillery for a number of days, and the last night the Americans threw up entrenchments; it was a misty, foggy night, rather wet but not rainy. Every soldier threw up for himself, as she understood, and she afterward saw and went into the entrenchments. Deponent's said husband was there throwing up entrenchments, and deponent cooked and carried in beef, and bread, and coffee (in a gallon pot) to the soldiers in the entrenchment.

On one occasion when deponent was thus employed carrying in provisions, she met General Washington, who asked her if she "was not afraid of the cannonballs"?

She replied, "No, the bullets would not cheat the gallows," that "It would not do for the men to fight and starve, too."

They dug entrenchments nearer and nearer to York-town every night or two till the last. While digging that, the enemy fired very heavy till about nine o'clock next morning, then stopped, and the drums from the enemy beat excessively. . . .

The drums continued beating, and all at once the officers hurrahed and swung their hats, and deponent asked them, "What is the matter now?"

One of them replied, "Are not you soldier enough to know what it means?"

Deponent replied, "No."

They then replied, "The British have surrendered."

Deponent, having provisions ready, carried the same down to the entrenchments that morning, and four of the soldiers whom she was in the habit of cooking for ate their breakfasts.

Deponent stood on one side of the road and the American officers upon the other side when the British officers came out of the town and rode up to the American officers and delivered up their swords, which the deponent thinks were returned again, and the British officers rode right on before the army, who marched out beating and playing a melancholy tune, their drums covered with black handkerchiefs and their fifes with black ribbons tied around them, into an old field and there grounded their arms and then returned into town again to await their destiny. Deponent recollects seeing a great many American officers, some on horseback and some on foot, but cannot call them all by name. Washington, Lafayette, and Clinton were among the number. The British general at the head of the army was a large, portly man, full face, and the tears rolled down his cheeks as he passed along. She does not recollect his name, but it was not Cornwallis.[1] She saw the latter afterward and noticed his being a man of **diminutive**[2] appearance and having cross eyes.

On going into town, she noticed two dead Negroes lying by the market house. She had the curiosity to go into a large building that stood nearby, and there she noticed the cupboards smashed to pieces and china dishes and other ware strewed around upon the floor, and among the rest a pewter cover to a hot basin that had a handle on it. She picked it up, supposing it to belong to the British, but the governor came in and claimed it as his, but said he would have the name of giving it away as it was the last one out of twelve that he could see, and accordingly presented it to deponent, and she afterward brought it home with her to Orange County and sold it for old pewter, which she has a hundred times regretted.

---

[1] Cornwallis—British General Charles Cornwallis, humiliated by defeat, pleaded ill and sent General Charles O'Hara to surrender to Washington before the combined American and French armies.

[2] **diminutive**—extremely small.

QUESTIONS TO CONSIDER

1. How important do you think the role played by Sarah Osborn (and others like her) was during the war? Explain.

2. What is Sarah Osborn's tone?

3. Why do you think Sarah Osborn "a hundred times regretted" selling the pewter cover?

Forming a New
Government

Chapter 4

The Articles of Confederation

BY A COMMITTEE OF DELEGATES FROM THE CONTINENTAL CONGRESS

The Continental Congress appointed one delegate from each state to form a Confederation Congress whose work was to draft a governing document for the new nation. The document established some important principles. It gave citizens of any state the rights and privileges of all the states. It said only agents of the Congress could represent the nation in negotiations with other nations. And it took first steps toward establishing a supreme court. Yet the document had weaknesses. It gave each state an equal voice, which angered the larger states. It said Congress can seek money and supplies from the states, but provided no way of enforcing its acts. There was no chief executive officer other than the president of the Congress. Nonetheless, it was a beginning.

To all to whom these Presents shall come, we the undersigned Delegates of the States affixed to our Names, send greeting.

Whereas the Delegates of the United States of America, in Congress assembled, did, on the 15th day of November, in the year [1777] . . . agree to certain Articles of Confederation and perpetual Union between the States of . . . in the words following, viz.:

Articles of Confederation and perpetual Union between the states of New Hampshire, Massachusetts-Bay, Rhode Island and Providence Plantations, Connecticut, New-York, New-Jersey, Pennsylvania, Delaware, Maryland, Virginia, North-Carolina, South-Carolina, and Georgia.

I. The stile of this Confederacy shall be "The United States of America."

II. Each state retains its sovereignty, freedom, and independence, and every power, jurisdiction, and right, which is not by this Confederation expressly delegated to the United States, in Congress assembled.

III. The said states hereby severally enter into a firm league of friendship with each other, for their common defence, the security of their liberties, and their mutual and general welfare, binding themselves to assist each other, against all force offered to, or attacks made upon them, or any of them, on account of religion, sovereignty, trade, or any other pretence whatever.

IV. The better to secure and perpetuate mutual friendship and intercourse among the people of the different states in this union, the free inhabitants of each of these states, paupers, vagabonds, and fugitives from justice excepted, shall be entitled to all privileges and immunities of free citizens in the several states; and the people of each state shall have free **ingress**[1] and **regress**[2] to and from any other state, and shall enjoy therein all

---

[1] **ingress**—right or permission to enter.

[2] **regress**—return.

the privileges of trade and commerce, subject to the same duties, impositions and restrictions as the inhabitants thereof respectively, provided that such restriction shall not extend so far as to prevent the removal of property imported into any state, to any other state, of which the owner is an inhabitant; provided also that no imposition, duties or restriction shall be laid by any state, on the property of the United States, or either of them.

If any person guilty of, or charged with treason, felony, or other high misdemeanor in any state, shall flee from justice, and be found in any of the United States, he shall, upon demand of the Governor or executive power of the state from which he fled, be delivered up and removed to the state having jurisdiction of his offence.

Full faith and credit shall be given in each of these states to the records, acts, and judicial proceedings of the courts and magistrates of every other state.

V. For the more convenient management of the general interests of the United States, delegates shall be annually appointed in such manner as the legislature of each state shall direct, to meet in Congress on the first Monday in November, in every year, with a power reserved to each state to recall its delegates, or any of them, at any time within the year, and to send others in their stead for the remainder of the year.

No state shall be represented in Congress by less than two, nor by more than seven members; and no person shall be capable of being a delegate for more than three years in any term of six years; nor shall any person, being a delegate, be capable of holding any office under the United States, for which he, or another for his benefit receives any salary, fees, or **emolument**[3] of any kind.

---

[3] **emolument**—payment for an office or employment; compensation.

Each state shall maintain its own delegates in a meeting of the states, and while they act as members of the committee of the states.

In determining questions in the United States in Congress assembled, each state shall have one vote.

Freedom of speech and debate in Congress shall not be impeached or questioned in any court or place out of Congress, and the members of Congress shall be protected in their persons from arrests and imprisonments, during the time of their going to and from, and attendance on Congress, except for treason, felony, or breach of the peace.

VI. No state, without the consent of the United States in Congress assembled, shall send any embassy to, or receive any embassy from, or enter into any conference, agreement, alliance, or treaty with any king, prince, or state; nor shall any person holding any office of profit or trust under the United States, or any of them, accept of any present, emolument, office, or title of any kind whatever from any king, prince, or foreign state; nor shall the United States in Congress assembled, or any of them, grant any title of nobility.

No two or more states shall enter into any treaty, confederation or alliance whatever between them, without the consent of the United States in Congress assembled, specifying accurately the purposes for which the same is to be entered into, and how long it shall continue.

No state shall lay any **imposts**[4] or duties, which may interfere with any stipulations in treaties, entered into by the United States in Congress assembled, with any king, prince, or state, in pursuance of any treaties already proposed by Congress, to the courts of France and Spain.

---

[4] **imposts**—things—such as taxes or duties—that are imposed.

No vessels of war shall be kept up in time of peace by any state, except such number only, as shall be deemed necessary by the United States in Congress assembled, for the defence of such state, or its trade; nor shall any body of forces be kept up by any state in time of peace, except such number only, as in the judgment of the United States in Congress assembled, shall be deemed requisite to garrison the forts necessary for the defence of such state; but every state shall always keep up a well regulated and disciplined militia, sufficiently armed and **accoutred**,[5] and shall provide and constantly have ready for use, in public stores, a due number of field pieces and tents, and a proper quantity of arms, ammunition, and camp equipage.

No state shall engage in any war without the consent of the United States in Congress assembled, unless such state be actually invaded by enemies, or shall have received certain advice of a resolution being formed by some nation of Indians to invade such state, and the danger is so imminent as not to admit of a delay till the United States in Congress assembled can be consulted: nor shall any state grant commissions to any ships or vessels of war, nor letters of marque or reprisal,[6] except it be after a declaration of war by the United States in Congress assembled, and then only against the kingdom or state and the subjects thereof, against which war has been so declared, and under such regulations as shall be established by the United States in Congress assembled, unless such state be infested by pirates, in which case vessels of war may be fitted out for that occasion, and kept so long as the danger shall continue, or until the United States in Congress assembled, shall determine otherwise.

---

[5] **accoutred**—outfitted and equipped, as for military duty.

[6] letters of marque or reprisal—licenses to outfit ships for capturing enemy merchant vessels.

VII. When land-forces are raised by any state for the common defence, all officers of or under the rank of colonel, shall be appointed by the legislature of each state respectively, by whom such forces shall be raised, or in such manner as such state shall direct, and all vacancies shall be filled up by the state which first made the appointment.

VIII. All charges of war, and all other expences that shall be incurred for the common defence or general welfare, and allowed by the United States in Congress assembled, shall be defrayed out of a common treasury, which shall be supplied by the several states in proportion to the value of all land within each state, granted to or surveyed for any person, as such land and the buildings and improvements thereon shall be estimated according to such mode as the United States in Congress assembled, shall from time to time direct and appoint.

The taxes for paying that proportion shall be laid and levied by the authority and direction of the legislatures of the several states within the time agreed upon by the United States in Congress assembled.

IX. The United States in Congress assembled, shall have the sole and exclusive right and power of determining on peace and war, except in the cases mentioned in the sixth article—of sending and receiving ambassadors—entering into treaties and alliances, provided that no treaty of commerce shall be made whereby the legislative power of the respective states shall be restrained from imposing such imposts and duties on foreigners, as their own people are subjected to, or from prohibiting the exportation or importation of any species of goods or commodities whatsoever—of establishing rules for deciding in all cases, what captures on land or water shall be legal, and in what manner prizes taken by land or naval forces in the service of the United

States shall be divided or appropriated—of granting letters of marque and reprisal in times of peace—appointing courts for the trial of piracies and felonies committed on the high seas and establishing courts for receiving and determining finally appeals in all cases of captures, provided that no member of Congress shall be appointed a judge of any of the said courts.

The United States in Congress assembled shall also be the last resort on appeal in all disputes and differences now subsisting or that hereafter may arise between two or more states concerning boundary, jurisdiction, or any other cause whatever; which authority shall always be exercised in the manner following. Whenever the legislative or executive authority or lawful agent of any state in controversy with another shall present a petition to Congress stating the matter in question and praying for a hearing, notice thereof shall be given by order of Congress to the legislative or executive authority of the other state in controversy, and a day assigned for the appearance of the parties by their lawful agents, who shall then be directed to appoint by joint consent, commissioners or judges to constitute a court for hearing and determining the matter in question: but if they cannot agree, Congress shall name three persons out of each of the United States, and from the list of such persons each party shall alternately strike out one, the petitioners beginning, until the number shall be reduced to thirteen; and from that number not less than seven, nor more than nine names as Congress shall direct, shall in the presence of Congress be drawn out by lot, and the persons whose names shall be so drawn or any five of them, shall be commissioners or judges, to hear and finally determine the controversy, so always as a major part of the judges who shall hear the cause shall agree in the determination: and if either party shall neglect to attend at the day appointed, without showing reasons, which Congress shall judge sufficient, or being present shall refuse to strike, the Congress shall proceed to nominate three persons out of each state, and the secretary of Congress shall strike in behalf of such party absent or refusing; and the judgment and sentence of the court to be appointed, in the manner before prescribed, shall be final and conclusive; and if any of the parties shall refuse to submit to the authority of such court, or to appear or defend their claim or cause, the court shall nevertheless proceed to pronounce sentence, or judgment, which shall in like manner be final and decisive, the judgment or sentence and other proceedings being in either case transmitted to Congress and lodged among the acts of Congress for the security of the parties concerned: provided that every commissioner, before he sits in judgment, shall take an oath to be administered by one of the judges of the supreme or superior court of the state, where the cause shall be tried, "well and truly to hear and determine the matter in question, according to the best of his judgment, without favour, affection, or hope of reward": provided also, that no state shall be deprived of territory for the benefit of the United States.

All controversies concerning the private right of soil claimed under different grants of two or more states, whose jurisdictions as they may respect such lands, and the states which passed such grants are adjusted, the said grants or either of them being at the same time claimed to have originated antecedent to such settlement of jurisdiction, shall on the petition of either party to the Congress of the United States, be finally determined as near as may be in the same manner as is before prescribed for deciding disputes respecting territorial jurisdiction between different states.

The United States in Congress assembled shall also have the sole and exclusive right and power of regulating the alloy and value of coin struck by their own authority, or by that of the respective states—fixing the standard of weights and measures throughout the United States—regulating the trade and managing all affairs with the Indians, not members of any of the states, provided that the legislative right of any state within its own limits be not infringed or violated—establishing or regulating post-offices from one state to another, throughout all the United States, and exacting such postage on the papers passing thro' the same as may be requisite to defray the expences of the said office—appointing all officers of the land forces, in the service of the United States, excepting regimental officers—appointing all the officers of the naval forces, and commissioning all officers whatever in the service of the United States—making rules for the government and regulation of the said land and naval forces, and directing their operations.

The United States in Congress assembled shall have authority to appoint a committee, to sit in the recess of Congress, to be denominated "A Committee of the States," and to consist of one delegate from each state; and to appoint such other committees and civil officers as may be necessary for managing the general affairs of the United States under their direction—to appoint one of their number to preside, provided that no person be allowed to serve in the office of president more than one year in any term of three years; to ascertain the necessary sums of money to be raised for the service of the United States, and to appropriate and apply the same for defraying the public expences—to borrow money, or emit bills on the credit of the United States, transmitting every half-year to the respective states an account of the sums of money so borrowed or emitted—to build and equip a navy—to agree upon the number of land forces, and to make requisitions from each state for its quota, in proportion to the number of white inhabitants in such state; which requisition shall be binding, and thereupon the legislature of each state shall appoint the regimental officers, raise the men and cloath,[7] arm, and equip them in a soldier-like manner, at the expence of the United States; and the officers and men so cloathed, armed, and equipped shall march to the place appointed, and within the time agreed on by the United States in Congress assembled. But if the United States in Congress assembled shall, on consideration of circumstances, judge proper that any state should not raise men, or should raise a smaller number than its quota, and that any other state should raise a greater number of men than the quota thereof, such extra number shall be raised, officered, cloathed, armed, and equipped in the same manner as the quota of such state, unless the legislature of such state shall judge that such extra number cannot be safely spared out of the same, in which case they shall raise, officer, cloath, arm, and equip as many of such extra number as they judge can be safely spared. And the officers and men so cloathed, armed, and equipped, shall march to the place appointed, and within the time agreed on by the United States in Congress assembled.

The United States in Congress assembled shall never engage in a war, nor grant letters of marque and reprisal in time of peace, nor enter into any treaties or alliances, nor coin money, nor regulate the value thereof, nor ascertain the sums and expences necessary for the defence and welfare of the United States, or any of them, nor emit bills, nor borrow money on the credit of the United States, nor appropriate money, nor agree upon the number of vessels of war, to be

---

[7] cloath—clothe.

built or purchased, or the number of land or sea forces to be raised, nor appoint a commander in chief of the army or navy, unless nine states assent to the same: nor shall a question on any other point, except for adjourning from day to day, be determined, unless by the votes of a majority of the United States in Congress assembled.

The Congress of the United States shall have power to adjourn to any time within the year, and to any place within the United States, so that no period of adjournment be for a longer duration than the space of six months, and shall publish the journal of their proceedings monthly, except such parts thereof relating to treaties, alliances or military operations, as in their judgment require secrecy; and the yeas and nays of the delegates of each state on any question shall be entered on the journal, when it is desired by any delegate; and the delegates of a state, or any of them, at his or their request shall be furnished with a transcript of the said journal, except such parts as are above excepted, to lay before the legislatures of the several states.

X. The Committee of the States, or any nine of them, shall be authorized to execute, in the recess of Congress, such of the powers of Congress as the United States in Congress assembled, by the consent of nine states, shall from time to time think expedient to vest them with; provided that no power be delegated to the said Committee, for the exercise of which, by the Articles of Confederation, the voice of nine states in the Congress of the United States assembled is requisite.

XI. Canada acceding to this confederation, and joining in the measures of the United States, shall be admitted into, and entitled to all the advantages of this union: but no other colony shall be admitted into the same, unless such admission be agreed to by nine states.

XII. All bills of credit emitted, monies borrowed, and debts contracted by, or under the authority of Congress, before the assembling of the United States, in pursuance of the present confederation, shall be deemed and considered as a charge against the United States, for payment and satisfaction whereof the said United States, and the public faith are hereby solemnly pledged.

XIII. Every state shall abide by the determination of the United States in Congress assembled, on all questions which by this confederation are submitted to them. And the Articles of this Confederation shall be inviolably observed by every state, and the union shall be perpetual; nor shall any alteration at any time hereafter be made in any of them; unless such alteration be agreed to in a Congress of the United States, and be afterwards confirmed by the legislatures of every state.

And Whereas it hath pleased the Great Governor of the World to incline the hearts of the legislatures we respectively represent in Congress, to approve of, and to authorize us to ratify the said articles of confederation and perpetual union. Know Ye that we the undersigned delegates, by virtue of the power and authority to us given for that purpose, do by these presents, in the name and in behalf of our respective constituents, fully and entirely ratify and confirm each and every of the said articles of confederation and perpetual union, and all and singular the matters and things therein contained: And we do further solemnly plight and engage the faith of our respective constituents, that they shall abide by the determinations of the United States in Congress assembled, on all questions, which by the said confederation are submitted to them. And that the articles thereof shall be inviolably observed by the states we respectively represent, and that the union shall be perpetual. In Witness whereof we have hereunto set our hands in Congress. Done at Philadelphia in the state of Pennsylvania the ninth day of July, in the year of our Lord one Thousand seven Hundred and Seventy-eight, and in the third year of the independence of America.

QUESTIONS TO CONSIDER

1. What was the purpose of the Articles of Confederation?

2. Why do you think it became a problem that the Articles of Confederation did not specify an executive branch or President?

3. What do you imagine was the greatest accomplishment of the Articles of Confederation?

"There Never Was a Good War or a Bad Peace"

BY BENJAMIN FRANKLIN

*Franklin, next to Washington, was the most well-known figure of
the era. He was the writer and publisher of* Poor Richard's
Almanac, *as well as a student of science, experimenter with elec-
tricity, inventor of the Franklin stove, and a major figure in
every activity of the founding of the nation. Franklin represented
the colonies and their interests to Parliament in London. He was
a delegate to the Continental Congress. He was on the committee
that wrote the Declaration of Independence. He traveled to France
to gain support for the Revolution. He negotiated the treaty in
which Great Britain recognized the thirteen colonies as an independent nation, and he helped to frame the Constitution. The
following brief excerpt is from a letter Franklin wrote to a friend
on July 27, 1783.*

Passy, July 27, 1783

I join with you most cordially in rejoicing at the return of peace. I hope it will be lasting, and that mankind will at length, as they call themselves reasonable creatures, have reason and sense enough to settle their differences without cutting throats; for, in my opinion, *there never was a good war or a bad peace.* What vast additions to the conveniences and comforts of living might mankind have acquired, if the money spent in wars had been employed in works of public utility! What an extension of agriculture, even to the tops of our mountains; what rivers rendered navigable or joined by canals; what bridges, aqueducts, new roads and other public works, edifices and improvements, rendering England a complete paradise, might have been obtained by spending those millions in doing good which in the last war have been spent in doing mischief; in bringing misery into thousands of families, and destroying the lives of so many thousands of working people, who might have performed the useful labor!

QUESTIONS TO CONSIDER

1. Do you agree with Benjamin Franklin that "there never was a good war or a bad peace"? Explain.

2. Are Franklin's views on war and peace relevant to modern-day nations and conflicts? Explain why or why not.

"I Retire from the Great Theatre of Action"

BY GENERAL GEORGE WASHINGTON

Peace talks had begun in 1782, and by September 1783, the negotiations were complete: The Treaty of Paris, officially ending the war, was signed. On December 23, General Washington addressed Congress.

Mr. President:

The great events on which my resignation depended having at length taken place; I have now the honor of offering my sincere Congratulations to Congress and of presenting myself before them to surrender into their hands the trust committed to me, and to claim the indulgence of retiring from the Service of my Country.

Happy in the confirmation of our Independence and Sovereignty, and pleased with the opportunity afforded the United States of becoming a respectable Nation, I resign with satisfaction the Appointment I accepted with **diffidence.**[1] A diffidence in my abilities to accomplish so arduous a task, which however was superseded by a confidence in the rectitude of our Cause, the support of the Supreme Power of the Union, and the patronage of Heaven.

The Successful termination of the War has verified the most **sanguine**[2] expectations, and my gratitude for the **interposition**[3] of Providence, and the assistance I have received from my Countrymen, increases with every review of the momentous Contest.

While I repeat my obligations to the Army in general, I should do injustice to my own feelings not to acknowledge in this place the peculiar Services and distinguished merits of the Gentlemen who have been attached to my person during the War. It was impossible the choice of confidential Officers to compose my family should have been more fortunate. Permit me Sir, to recommend in particular those, who have continued in Service to the present moment, as worthy of the favorable notice and patronage of Congress.

I consider it an indispensable duty to close this last solemn act of my Official life, by commending the Interests of our dearest Country to the protection of Almighty God, and those who have the superintendence of them, to his holy keeping.

Having now finished the work assigned me, I retire from the great theatre of Action; and bidding an Affectionate farewell to this August body under whose orders I have so long acted, I here offer my Commission, and take my leave of all the employments of public life.

---

[1] **diffidence**—timid reluctance.

[2] **sanguine**—optimistic.

[3] **interposition**—intervention.

QUESTIONS TO CONSIDER

1. What is ironic about the last sentence of General Washington's resignation?

2. What does Washington have to say about the men who served with him?

3. Does Washington seem sad to be resigning his commission? Support your answer.

Delegates to the Constitutional Convention

BY FRED BARBASH

In 1786, only five states sent delegates to a convention to solve the country's trade crisis. James Madison, Alexander Hamilton, and others then proposed a convention in Philadelphia to "adjust" the federal system. Shays's Rebellion made it even more clear that the Articles of Confederation did not provide an effective government. Riots spread across the Northeast. Congress, with no army and no money, was helpless to put down the rebellion. The proposal was accepted. The states chose their delegates to a Convention to revise the Articles of Confederation. Fred Barbash describes the men who came to Philadelphia in May 1787.

Madison took soundings as the delegates arrived in Philadelphia, and he was pleased with what he heard. They might not yet agree on a solution, he found, but there was no doubt they shared his view of the severity of the problem. . . .

Looking at the list of delegates, he had every reason to be satisfied, even to gloat over what was really his first major victory.

In Pennsylvania a powerful and tremendously popular party called "radicals" held considerable political sway, particularly among ordinary people. But this group was unrepresented in the state's delegation, which was dominated by their archenemies: Robert Morris, Gouverneur Morris, James Wilson—wealthy businessmen and lawyers.

Massachusetts too had a significant popular party, strongest in the western reaches of the state. But its delegation came entirely from Boston and the East, from the "codfish aristocracy."

The South Carolinians came exclusively from Charleston, representing the state's low-country planters, the famous South Carolina "**oligarchy**,"[1] but not the restless people of the outlying reaches. All of the delegates chosen by South Carolina were related to one another, by blood or marriage.

The same was true of virtually all the delegations. Absent were the names of many strong leaders identified with paper money or with the rights of the states, men whose views differed sharply from Madison's brand of nationalism; men like Patrick Henry of Virginia, . . . John Hancock of Massachusetts and Willie Jones of North Carolina. These men were formidable adversaries, skillful politicians, powerful orators, any one of whom was capable of affecting the course of events in Philadelphia.

No conspiracy in the selection process was evident, though perhaps if these men had known what Madison's plan of government contained they might have thought again about staying home. The lopsidedness was the result of self-selection: many of these men had had the chance to attend and turned it down.

---

[1] **oligarchy**—government by a few, especially by a small faction of persons or families.

In fact, the one state that might have really caused trouble boycotted the convention. Rhode Island. Rogue Island, its many enemies called it. Fools' Island. For most of the delegates, Rhode Island was the single best reason for having a convention in the first place. The state, in addition to craving paper money, was suspected of harboring fugitives from Shays's Rebellion.[2] Right-thinking men from Rhode Island felt compelled to apologize for their state, as in this letter from James M. Varnum to Washington on the eve of the convention:

> Permit me, Sir, to observe that the measures of our present legislature do not exhibit the real character of the state. They are equally **reprobated**,[3] & abhor'd by Gentlemen of the learned professions, by the whole mercantile body, & by most of the respectable farmers and mechanicks. . . .

All told, there were during the course of the convention fifty-five delegates in attendance—though never at one time.

From Massachusetts:

Elbridge Gerry, forty-three, merchant.
Nathaniel Gorham, forty-eight, businessman,
   president of the Congress.
Rufus King, thirty-two, lawyer, congressman.
Caleb Strong, forty-two, lawyer.

From New Hampshire:

Nicholas Gilman, thirty-one, congressman.

---

[2] Shays's Rebellion—in 1786, several hundred Western Massachusetts farmers, armed with pitch forks, marched on the Springfield Arsenal to get weapons. Daniel Shays, a former captain in the Revolutionary Army, was their leader. Unable to pay their mortgages, the angry farmers wanted to prevent the courts from foreclosing on mortgages and taking away their farms.

[3] **reprobated**—condemned as morally unprincipled.

John Langdon, forty-five, businessman,
    former President of New Hampshire, congressman.

From Connecticut:
Oliver Ellsworth, forty-two, lawyer.
Roger Sherman: sixty-six, lawyer, mayor, congressman.
William Samuel Johnson: fifty-nine, lawyer, congressman.

From New York:
Alexander Hamilton, thirty or thirty-two, lawyer,
    former congressman.
John Lansing, Jr., thirty-three, lawyer, mayor of Albany.
Robert Yates, forty-nine, lawyer.

From New Jersey:
David Brearley, forty-one, chief justice,
    New Jersey Supreme Court.
Jonathan Dayton, twenty-six, lawyer, legislator.
William C. Houston, about forty-one, lawyer,
    former congressman.
William Livingston, sixty-three, lawyer, writer,
    governor of New Jersey.
William Paterson, forty-two, lawyer, former
    congressman.

From Pennsylvania:
George Clymer, forty-eight, merchant, legislator,
    former congressman.
Thomas Fitzsimons, forty-six, businessman,
    former congressman.
Benjamin Franklin, eighty-one, President of
    Pennsylvania, scientist, diplomat.
Robert Morris, fifty-three, businessman, former
    legislator, congressman and superintendent of
    finance of the Confederation.
Gouverneur Morris, thirty-five, lawyer, former
    congressman.

James Wilson, forty-four, lawyer, congressman.
Jared Ingersoll, thirty-seven, lawyer, former congressman.
Thomas Mifflin, forty-three, businessman, speaker of
the Pennsylvania legislature.

From Delaware:
Richard Bassett, forty-two, lawyer.
Gunning Bedford, Jr., forty, attorney general of Delaware.
Jacob Broom, thirty-five, businessman.
John Dickinson, fifty-four, lawyer, former congressman,
former President of Pennsylvania and Delaware.
George Read, fifty-three, lawyer.

From Maryland:
Daniel Carroll, fifty-seven, merchant, president of the
Maryland Senate.
Daniel of St. Thomas Jenifer, sixty-four, planter, former
president of the Maryland Senate and former
congressman.
Luther Martin, about thirty-nine, lawyer, attorney
general of Maryland.
James McHenry, thirty-four, physician, former congressman.
John F. Mercer, twenty-eight, congressman.

From Virginia:
John Blair, fifty-five, lawyer and judge.
James McClurg, physician.
James Madison, thirty-six, congressman.
George Mason, about sixty-two, planter.
Edmund J. Randolph, thirty-three, lawyer, Governor
of Virginia.
George Washington, fifty-five, farmer.
George Wythe, about sixty-one, lawyer, judge.

From North Carolina:
William Blount, thirty-eight, businessman, congressman.
William R. Davie, about thirty-one, lawyer.

Alexander Martin, about forty-seven, lawyer.
Richard D. Spaight, twenty-nine, Speaker of the
    North Carolina Assembly.
Hugh Williamson, fifty-two, scholar, lawyer, congressman.

From South Carolina:
Pierce Butler, forty-three, planter.
Charles Pinckney, twenty-nine, lawyer, congressman.
Charles Cotesworth Pinckney, forty-one, lawyer.
John Rutledge, forty-seven, lawyer, judge.

From Georgia:
Abraham Baldwin, thirty-two, lawyer, congressman.
William Few, thirty-eight, congressman.
William Houston, about thirty-two, lawyer.
William L. Pierce, about forty-seven, businessman,
    congressman.

The titles and occupations said little about them. There were fifty-five names, but there were a hundred or two hundred answers to the questions "What do you do?" and "Where do you come from?" Roger Sherman of Connecticut, for example, was a merchant, an almanac writer, a judge, a mayor, a surveyor and, once upon a time, a shoemaker. William Churchill Houston was a lawyer, a professor of mathematics and a member of the Continental Congress. Hugh Williamson of North Carolina had been variously a Presbyterian minister, a professor of mathematics and a physician. Charles Cotesworth Pinckney of South Carolina, in addition to being a lawyer and a general in the Continental Army, was an accomplished botanist.

As a group, they were extremely well educated, far more so than the population as a whole, and in those days educated meant educated: admission to the best American colleges required young men at the age of fourteen or fifteen to translate works of Greek and Latin. The schools most heavily represented were Princeton (eight including Madison), Yale (four), William and Mary (four), Harvard (three) and Columbia (two).

They were the sons of cobblers, the sons of lords, the sons of clothiers, planters, blacksmiths and barristers; the children of patriots, loyalists and royalists. Almost all were wealthy or at least comfortable, and those who hadn't started out that way had become so, for all of them were constantly looking to improve their lot. Whether they chose land speculation, trade, manufacture or law, they subscribed to the tenet that in improving themselves they would also improve the country. Ambition was patriotic. . . .

They had come to Philadelphia to frame a constitution. For this task they were unquestionably qualified. Thirty of them had done this sort of thing at least once before, as participants in conventions called to draft state constitutions, and all but a few had served in state legislatures. They had no need for aides to tell them what to say and think. There would be no need for a staff.

Service in Congress was the unifying experience. At least forty-one of the fifty-five had served some time in the Congress, and many had devoted years to it. This was the place where they first encountered men from different states and different regions; this was the place where men became continentalists. This was the place that brought together characters as different as the pious New Englander Sherman and the high-living and exceedingly impious Gouverneur Morris; the self-confident and brash Hamilton and the shy and scholarly Madison. Over the years, though they disagreed on many points, the men devoted to the Congress had become a kind of brotherhood.

Many had been there in '76, for the break with England, and for the tension before the Declaration while Jefferson, Franklin, Sherman and the others went behind closed doors to draft it. Many had left Congress to fight the war. Others had stayed to help manage it, for there was no vast bureaucracy to do it for them. They personally gave Washington his orders; they personally had to figure out how to find the tents, the blankets, the powder and the troops. Nor was there such a thing as a safe distance: they fled for their lives during the battle for Philadelphia in '77 as the British captured the city.

Never would any of them forget the day the courier arrived with news of the surrender at Yorktown. The doorkeeper of Congress, an aged man, died suddenly, Dr. Benjamin Rush later reported, "immediately after hearing of the capture of Lord Cornwallis's army. His death was universally ascribed to a violent emotion of political joy. . . ."

Many of the delegates had shared powerful and indelible experiences. But each man brought with him his own political calculus. Every proposal, every clause, every semicolon and comma, would be scrutinized for its impact on region, on state, on class, and this would determine the outcome of the convention. For these men were politicians, and the convention, whatever else it was to be, was, above all, about politics.

The calculation began in earnest even before the first item of business was brought to the floor. Gouverneur Morris and Robert Morris (they were not related) approached the Virginians to convince them to cut the small states down to size in the convention by having votes cast according to the size of each state, rather than giving all states equal votes. Madison stifled the idea. He wanted to soften up the small states, not enrage them.

Meanwhile, some of the small-state delegates in town had caught a glimpse of one of the proposals for a new government. It wasn't Madison's, but it might as well have been, for, like Madison's plan, it proposed a Congress based not on equality of the states but on the size of the states. The principle by which each state had one vote in the government would be replaced by proportional representation, allowing the large states to dominate.

Upon reading it, George Read of Delaware immediately wrote to Dickinson, who had not yet arrived:

> I am in possession of a copied draft of a federal system intended to be proposed. . . . By this plan our state may have a representation . . . of one member in eighty. . . . I suspect it to be of importance to the small states that their deputies should keep a strict watch upon the movements and propositions from the larger states, who will probably combine to swallow up the smaller ones by addition, division or impoverishment. . . . If you have any wish to assist in guarding such attempts, you will be speedy in your attendance.

Read had known instinctively that this was coming and had already taken defensive measures, making sure that the official instructions of the Delaware delegates included a provision requiring them to walk out of the convention if it aimed to wipe out state equality.

On opening day, as the instructions of each state from its legislature were read, Delaware's stood out ominously.

QUESTIONS TO CONSIDER

1. Why do many of the delegates refer to Rhode Island as "Rogue Island"?

2. What makes these delegates "unquestionably qualified" to frame a constitution?

3. Why are the delegates from Delaware so upset?

Slavery: "A Practice Totally Repugnant"

BY PATRICK HENRY, THOMAS PAINE, AND HENRY LAURENS

When most colonists used language about slavery to describe their situation with Britain, they were merely employing a strong metaphor. They were not thinking about the plight of the slaves in their society at all. But some Patriots recognized the irony of slavery in the midst of "an enlightened age."

Letter to Robert Pleasants
by Patrick Henry

Hanover, January 18, 1773

Dear Sir: I take this opportunity to acknowledge the receipt of Anthony Benezet's book against the slave trade. I thank you for it. It is not a little surprising that the professors of Christianity, whose chief excellence consists in softening the human heart and in cherishing and improving its finer feelings, should encourage a practice so totally **repugnant**[1] to the first impressions of right and wrong. What adds to the wonder is that this abominable practice has been introduced in the most enlightened ages. Times that seem to have pretensions to boast of high improvements in the arts and sciences, and refined morality, have brought into general use, and guarded by many laws, a species of violence and tyranny which our more rude and **barbarous,**[2] but more honest ancestors detested. Is it not amazing that at a time when the rights of humanity are defined and understood with precision, in a country, above all others, fond of liberty, that in such an age and in such a country we find men professing a religion the most humane, mild, gentle and generous, adopting a principle as repugnant to humanity as it is inconsistent with the Bible, and destructive to liberty? Every thinking, honest man rejects it in speculation; how few in practice from conscientious motives!

Would anyone believe I am the master of slaves of my own purchase! I am drawn along by the general inconvenience of living here without them. I will not, I cannot justify it. However **culpable**[3] my conduct, I will so far pay my devoir to virtue as to own the excellence and **rectitude**[4] of her precepts, and lament my want of conformity to them.

I believe a time will come when an opportunity will be offered to abolish this **lamentable**[5] evil. Everything we do is to improve it, if it happens in our day; if not, let us transmit to our descendants, together with our slaves, a pity for their unhappy lot and an abhorrence of

---

[1] **repugnant**—repulsive.

[2] **barbarous**—cruel.

[3] **culpable**—deserving of blame or censure.

[4] **rectitude**—moral uprightness; righteousness.

[5] **lamentable**—regrettable; deplorable.

slavery. If we cannot reduce this wished-for reformation to practice, let us treat the unhappy victims with **lenity.**[6] It is the furthest advance we can make toward justice. It is a debt we owe to the purity of our religion, to show that it is at **variance**[7] with that law which warrants slavery.

I know not when to stop. I could say many things on the subject, a serious view of which gives a gloomy perspective to future times.

from the *Pennsylvania Journal* and *The Weekly Advertiser*
by Thomas Paine

March 8, 1775

The chief design of this paper is not to disprove [slavery], which many have sufficiently done; but to entreat Americans to consider:

1. With what consistency or decency they complain so loudly of attempts to enslave them, while they hold so many hundred thousands in slavery; and annually enslave many thousands more, without any pretence of authority, or claim upon them?

2. How just, how suitable to our crime is the punishment with which providence threatens us? We have enslaved multitudes, and shed much innocent blood in doing it; and now we are threatened with the same. And while other evils are confessed and **bewailed,**[8] why not this especially, and publicly; than which no other vice has brought so much guilt on the land?

---

[6] **lenity**—leniency.
[7] **variance**—in disagreement.
[8] **bewailed**—lamented.

3. Whether, then, all ought not immediately to discontinue and renounce it, with grief and abhorrence? Should not every society bear testimony against it, and account obstinate persisters in it bad men, enemies to their country, and exclude them from fellowship; as they often do for much lesser faults?

4. The great question may be—what should be done with those who are enslaved already? To turn the old and infirm free would be injustice and cruelty; they who enjoyed the labors of their better days should keep and treat them humanely. As to the rest, let prudent men, with the assistance of legislatures, determine what is practicable for masters, and best for them. Perhaps some could give them lands upon reasonable rent; some, employing them in their labor still, might give them some reasonable allowances for it; so as all may have some property, and fruits of their labors at their own disposal, and be encouraged to industry; the family may live together, and enjoy the natural satisfaction of exercising relative affections and duties, with civil protection and other advantages, like fellow men. Perhaps they may sometime form useful barrier settlements on the frontiers. Then they may become interested in the public welfare, and assist in promoting it; instead of being dangerous, as now they are, should any enemy promise them a better condition. . . .

Letter to John Laurens
by Henry Laurens

Charleston, S. C., 14th August, 1776

My Negroes, all to a man, are strongly attached to me; hitherto not one of them has attempted to desert; on the contrary, those who are more exposed hold themselves always ready to fly from the enemy in case of a sudden descent. Many hundreds of that colour have been stolen and decoyed by the servants of King George the Third. Captains of British ships of war and noble lords have busied themselves in such inglorious pilferage, to the disgrace of their master and disgrace of their cause. These Negroes were first enslaved by the English; acts of parliament have established the slave trade in favour of the home-residing English, and almost totally prohibited the Americans from reaping any share of it. Men of war, forts, castles, governors, companies and committees are employed and authorized by the English parliament to protect, regulate and extend the slave trade. Negroes are brought by Englishmen and sold as slaves to Americans. Bristol, Liverpool, Manchester, Birmingham, etc., etc., live upon the slave trade. The British parliament now employ their men-of-war to steal those Negroes from the Americans to whom they had sold them, pretending to set the poor wretches free, but basely trepan[9] and sell them into tenfold worse slavery in the West Indies, where probably they will become the property of Englishmen again, and of some who sit in parliament. What meanness! What complicated wickedness appears in this scene! O England, how changed! How fallen!

You know, my dear son, I abhor slavery. I was born in a country where slavery had been established by British kings and parliaments, as well as by the laws of that country ages before my existence. I found the Christian religion and slavery growing under the same authority and cultivation. I nevertheless disliked it. In former days there was no combating the prejudices of men supported by interest; the day I hope is approaching when, from principles of gratitude as well as justice, every man will strive to be foremost in showing his readiness to comply with the golden rule.

---

[9] trepan—trap; ensnare.

Not less than twenty thousand pounds sterling would all my Negroes produce if sold at public auction tomorrow. I am not the man who enslaved them; they are indebted to Englishmen for that favour; nevertheless I am devising means for **manumitting**[10] many of them, and for cutting off the entail of slavery. Great powers oppose me—the laws and customs of my country, my own and the **avarice**[11] of my countrymen. What will my children say if I deprive them of so much estate? These are difficulties, but not **insuperable**.[12] I will do as much as I can in my time, and leave the rest to a better hand.

---

[10] **manumitting**—freeing from slavery; emancipating.

[11] **avarice**—greed.

[12] **insuperable**—impossible to overcome; insurmountable.

QUESTIONS TO CONSIDER

1. Given Patrick Henry's stated views on slavery, is it surprising that he himself owns slaves? Explain.

2. Why does Thomas Paine think the time is right to abolish African-American slavery?

3. What do you imagine was the general reaction to Paine's speech?

4. Why are there difficulties, according to Laurens, involved in the freeing of slaves?

5. Who is the "better hand" that Laurens refers to in the final sentence?

Why the Constitution Didn't End Slavery

BY FRED BARBASH

Why didn't the Constitutional Convention end slavery? Many of the important figures of the day were opposed to slavery. Even as the delegates sat deliberating, an abolitionist convention in Philadelphia was also meeting. The abolitionists sent over a petition to end slavery. Yet, the "national sin" still was not erased. Constitutional student and journalist Fred Barbash explains. The following is from his book The Founding: A Dramatic Account of the Writing of the Constitution.

Charles Cotesworth Pinckney of South Carolina had bluntly told the convention that if the committee should fail to insert some "security to the Southern states" with regard to slavery, he "should be bound by duty" to his state to vote against the report.

The Committee of Detail, in response, had brought back a special clause for the Deep South. The last eight words of the clause were the crucial ones: "No tax or duty shall be laid by the legislature on articles exported from any state; nor on the migration or importation of such persons as the several states shall think proper to admit; *nor shall such migration or importation be prohibited.*"

The provision would make the slave trade untouchable by the national government. Slavery would be purely the business of each state.

It brought home a truth about the convention, one already taught by the small states. The states wanted union, all right, but their support was always conditional.

Each would exact a price. . . .

All the states had slaves at one point or another. But eight of them—the eight to the north—had so few in 1787 that slaves played a **negligible**[1] role in their economies. Massachusetts and Pennsylvania had already taken steps toward emancipation.

In Maryland, Virginia, the two Carolinas and Georgia, slavery thrived: their populations were two-thirds free and one-third slave. But Maryland and Virginia were already overstocked with slaves and no longer needed the slave traffic.

Thus the clause protecting the slave trade would benefit only the deepest South.

The debate began late in the afternoon of Tuesday, August 21.

Luther Martin [from Maryland] (who himself had a slave servant) rose. He had three points to make, and this time he did so succinctly.

Point one: The convention, he said, had previously approved the three-fifths formula, giving the South representation in the Congress for its slave population.

---

[1] **negligible**—not very important; slight.

Thus the South would have an incentive to continue the slave trade to enhance its political power.

Point two: Slavery, while confined to the South, was a burden on the entire country. Why? "Because slaves weaken one part of the Union which the other parts are bound to protect." He wasn't explicit, but everyone understood what he referred to: the prospect of slave insurrection, to which the armed forces of the entire Union would have to respond under the new Constitution.

The point was important. The Southerners claimed that slavery was a local matter. Not so, Martin was saying; it was a national concern.

Point three: "It is inconsistent with the principles of the Revolution and dishonorable to the American character to have such a feature in the Constitution."

Martin moved to allow either a tax on the importation of slaves, as a disincentive to the traffic, or outright prohibition of the trade. . . .

Rutledge [from South Carolina] responded to Martin point by point.

First: "I do not see how the importation of slaves could be encouraged by this section."

Second: "I am not apprehensive of insurrections and would readily exempt the other states from the obligation to protect" the South against them.

Third: "Religion and humanity have nothing to do with this question. Interest alone is the governing principle with nations. The true question at present is whether the Southern states shall or shall not be parties to the Union. If the Northern states consult their interest, they will not oppose the increase of slaves. . . ." It would benefit the North too, he said, for it would enhance the agricultural output of the South, and the Northern shipping industry would become the carriers of those crops.

Ellsworth of Connecticut was next. . . .

"Let every state import what it pleases," said Ellsworth. "The morality and wisdom of slavery are considerations belonging to the states themselves. What enriches a part enriches the whole, and the states are the best judges of their particular interest. The old Confederation has not meddled with this point, and I do not see any greater necessity for bringing it within the policy of the new one."

Charles Pinckney:

"South Carolina can never receive the plan if it prohibits the slave trade. In every proposed extension of the powers of Congress, that state has expressly and watchfully excepted that of meddling with the importation of Negroes. If the states be all left at liberty on this subject, South Carolina may perhaps by degrees do of herself what is wished [end the slave traffic], as Virginia and Maryland already have done. . . ."

The next day,. . . Roger Sherman [Connecticut] rose in support of Ellsworth.

Of course, Sherman hastened to say, he disapproved of the slave trade. "Yet as the states are now possessed of the right to import slaves, as the public good does not require it to be taken from them, and as it is expedient to have as few objections as possible to the proposed scheme of government, I think it best to leave the matter as we find it. . . ."

The Virginians

Virginia had been silent. For Washington, Madison, Mason and the others (including Jefferson, had he been there) this was a difficult moment, personally and politically. Slavery was the chink in their moral armor, the institution that made their crusade for individual liberty sound like hypocrisy. "Hypocrisy" was the wrong word. They actually believed what they said about slavery. They simply did not or could not act on it. Many of them had talked for years about manumitting their own slaves. It didn't happen. Here was a chance for a modest statement. What would it cost Virginia to oppose the clause? What would it cost Virginia if the slave traffic were prohibited? Very little.

Mason felt the dilemma deeply. His claim to fame was the Virginia Declaration of Rights and the words "All men are naturally equal." Yet he was among the largest, if not the largest, slaveholder in the room. . . .

. . . Mason broke Virginia's silence. His opening words were the same old Virginia song: Blame it on the British. "This infernal traffic originated in the avarice of British merchants. The British government constantly checked the attempts of Virginia to put a stop to it."

Then his tone changed. Slavery was not simply a local matter, he declared. It concerned the whole Union. Slave insurrections had taken place in Greece and Sicily. So why not here? And contrary to what the South Carolinians were telling them, the trade would not go away of its own accord. "The Western people are already calling out for slaves for their new lands and will fill that country with slaves if they can be got through South Carolina and Georgia."

Here was Mason, a Southerner to his bones, taking on the South and its most cherished institution. "Slavery discourages arts and manufactures. The poor despise labor when performed by slaves. They prevent the immigration of whites, who really enrich and strengthen a country. . . . "

Mason's speech, part confession, part prophecy, was an irresistible target. It was one thing to hear it from Luther Martin; wholly another to hear a lecture on the morality of slavery from the largest slaveholder in the room.

Oliver Ellsworth had heard just about enough.

"As I have never owned a slave," he replied to Mason, "I cannot judge of the effects of slavery on character. However, if it was to be considered in a moral light, we ought to go farther and free those already in the country."

Virginia and Maryland could afford to moralize, he went on. "Slaves multiply so fast in Virginia and Maryland that it is cheaper to raise than import them, whilst in the sickly rice swamps, foreign supplies are necessary." If we strike the clause, Ellsworth said, "we shall be unjust towards South Carolina and Georgia. Let us not intermeddle. As population increases, poor laborers will be so plenty as to render slaves useless. Slavery in time will not be a speck in our country.". . .

But one by one, as other delegates spoke, Mason's position picked up strength. They were beginning to understand that the slavery provisions could be seen as a blot on the Constitution.

Gerry [Massachusetts]:

"We have nothing to do with the conduct of the states as to slaves, but ought to be careful not to give any sanction to it. "

Dickinson [Delaware]:

It is "inadmissible on every principle of honor and safety that the importation of slaves should be authorized to the states by the Constitution. The true question is whether the national happiness would be promoted or impeded by the importation, and this question ought to be left to the national government, not to the states particularly interested."

. . . Rutledge delivered the South's response. Only one thing mattered and it was this:

"If the convention thinks that North Carolina, South Carolina and Georgia will ever agree to the plan, unless their right to import slaves be untouched, the expectation is in vain. The people of those states will never be such fools as to give up so important an interest."

Had a vote been taken at this point, it might have been close. On the other hand, how much, really, did the slave traffic matter to the Northern maritime states? As a matter of morality, maybe it did matter. As a matter of reality, probably not. What, after all, did Massachusetts or Connecticut have to lose by allowing the slave trade to continue? Was it worth risking the Constitution itself?

A negotiating point—the Navigation Acts

In that Committee of Detail report, however, there sat a clause that the maritime states truly loathed. It said: "No navigation act shall be passed without the assent of two thirds of the members present in each house." Navigation acts—laws requiring that all commodities be transported in ships belonging to a particular nation—were used by Britain to force Americans to ship their goods exclusively in British vessels. Americans hated navigation acts when applied to them. But when the acts were used by them, the potential gain for Northern shippers made New Englanders salivate.

For the same reason the shippers liked navigation acts, Southerners feared them, for they would allow the shippers to charge however much they pleased. . . .

Enter Gouverneur Morris.

He had studied the Committee of Detail report carefully. The slave traffic. Import duties. Navigation acts. They were all on the floor now. Perhaps this could be settled with a deal. Let all of these provisions be referred to a committee, he suggested. "These things may form a bargain among the Northern and Southern states."

It was late August. Three long months had gone by. The delegates were exhausted, anxious to get it over with. There was so much yet to be done. The convention went along with the committee idea. . . .

[Luther] Martin later described what happened in the committee.

I found the eastern States, notwithstanding their aversion to slavery, were very willing to indulge the southern states, at least with a temporary liberty to prosecute the slave-trade, provided the southern States would, in their turn, gratify them, by laying no restriction on navigation acts; and after a very little time the committee, by a great majority, agreed on a report, by which the general government was to be prohibited from preventing the importation of slaves for a limited time [until 1800] and the restrictive clause relative to navigation acts was to be omitted.

The Southerners also quickly agreed that a duty could be levied on the slave traffic—provided it wasn't too high.

On Saturday, August 25, the convention considered the deal. . . .

On every element, seven states—New Hampshire, Massachusetts, Connecticut, Maryland, North Carolina, South Carolina and Georgia—voted as one. For good measure, the year 1800 was changed to 1808, making it an even two decades before Congress could tamper with the slave trade.

There were a few protests.

Sherman and Madison objected to the duty to be allowed on slaves, as if they were a commodity. It would acknowledge in the Constitution of the United States of America that human beings were property.

This was the "price" of the rest of the deal, said King [Massachusetts] and Langdon [New Hampshire]. . . .

On August 29, . . . [Pierce Butler of South Carolina] had one other motion on his mind: "If any person bound to service or labor in any of the United States shall escape into another State, he or she shall not be discharged from such service or labor, in consequence of any regulations subsisting in the state to which they escape, but shall be delivered up to the person justly claiming their service or labor."

This was the "fugitive-slave clause." It was an exact replica of a clause inserted into the recently enacted congressional ordinance which had provided for the opening of the West. It would eliminate "free" states as sanctuary, as refuge for runaway slaves, for men seeking their freedom.

It passed, without dissent.

Then the second part of the deal, removing slavery from the realm of national power, was agreed to, unanimously.

The business was done.

QUESTIONS TO CONSIDER

1. For the Deep South, what was the importance of the last eight words of the Committee of Detail's special clause?

2. What does Luther Martin mean when he says that slavery is a "national concern"?

3. What was the compromise that settled the debate about the slave trade?

4. What was the fugitive-slave clause?

5. Why didn't the Constitutional Convention end slavery? Explain in your own words.

Federalist Papers
(Number 10)

BY JAMES MADISON AS "PUBLIUS"

James Madison, who would later become the fourth President of the United States, was the driving force behind the Constitution. A Virginia landowner, he was elected to the Continental Congress in 1780. By this time he already had established himself as a strong Patriot. In Virginia's Revolutionary Convention he drafted the guarantee of religious freedom. It is he who persuaded a strong states-rights delegate, John Tyler, to sponsor the proposal for a convention to adjust the Articles of Confederation. It was he who formulated the Virginia Plan, which provided the basis for the Constitution. To help energize public opinion in support of ratification, he worked with Alexander Hamilton and John Jay on the Federalist Papers. This series of essays spelled out the reasons why each of the different elements of the Constitution should be supported. In the selection below, Madison explains the advantages of representative government.

[I]t may be concluded that a pure democracy, by which I mean a society, consisting of a small number of citizens, who assemble and administer the government in person, can admit of no cure for the mischiefs of faction. A common passion or interest will, in almost every case, be felt by a majority of the whole; a communication and concert results from the form of government itself; and there is nothing to check the inducements to sacrifice the weaker party, or an obnoxious individual. Hence it is, that such democracies have ever been spectacles of turbulence and contention; have ever been found incompatible with personal security, or the rights of property; and have in general been as short in their lives, as they have been violent in their deaths. Theoretic politicians, who have patronized this species of government, have **erroneously**[1] supposed, that by reducing mankind to a perfect equality in their political rights, they would, at the same time, be perfectly equalized, and assimilated in their possessions, their opinions, and their passions.

A republic, by which I mean a government in which the scheme of representation takes place, opens a different prospect, and promises the cure for which we are seeking. Let us examine the points in which it varies from pure democracy and we shall comprehend both the nature of the cure, and the **efficacy**[2] which it must derive from the union.

The two great points of difference between a democracy and a republic, are first, the delegation of the government, in the latter, to a small number of citizens elected by the rest; secondly, the greater number of citizens, and greater sphere of country, over which the latter may be extended.

The effect of the first difference is, on the one hand, to refine and enlarge the public views, by passing them through the medium of a chosen body of citizens, whose wisdom may best discern the true interest of their country, and whose patriotism and love of justice, will be least

---

[1] **erroneously**—mistakenly.

[2] **efficacy**—power to produce an effect.

likely to sacrifice it to temporary or partial considerations. Under such a regulation, it may well happen that the public voice pronounced by the representatives of the people, will be more consonant to the public good, than if pronounced by the people themselves convened for the purpose. On the other hand, the effect may be inverted. Men of **factious**[3] tempers, of local prejudices, or of sinister designs, may by intrigue, by corruption, or by other means, first obtain the **suffrages,**[4] and then betray the interests of the people. The question resulting is, whether small or extensive republics are most favourable to the election of proper guardians of the public **weal;**[5] and it is clearly decided in favour of the latter by two obvious considerations.

In the first place it is to be remarked, that however small the republic may be, the representatives must be raised to a certain number, in order to guard against the **cabals**[6] of a few; and that however large it may be, they must be limited to a certain number, in order to guard against the confusion of a multitude. Hence the number of representatives in the two cases not being in proportion to that of the constituents, and being proportionally greatest in the small republic, it follows, that if the proportion of fit characters be not less in the large than in the small republic, the former will present a greater opinion, and consequently a greater probability of a fit choice.

In the next place, as each representative will be chosen by a greater number of citizens in the large than in the small republic, it will be more difficult for unworthy candidates to practise with success the vicious arts, by which elections are too often carried; and the suffrages

---

[3] **factious**—divisive; relating to factions or groups within a government that are self-seeking.

[4] **suffrages**—votes.

[5] **weal**—well-being.

[6] **cabals**—groups secretly united to gain power in public affairs.

of the people being more free, will be more likely to centre on men who possess the most attractive merit, and the most diffusive and established characters.

It must be confessed, that in this, as in most other cases, there is a mean, on both sides of which inconveniences will be found to lie. By enlarging too much the number of electors, you render the representative too little acquainted with all their local circumstances and lesser interests; as by reducing it too much, you render him unduly attached to these, and too little fit to comprehend and pursue great and national objects. The federal constitution forms a happy combination in this respect; the great and **aggregate**[7] interests being referred to the national, the local and particular to the state legislatures.

The other point of difference is, the greater number of citizens and extent of territory which may be brought within the compass of republican, than of democratic government; and it is this circumstance principally which renders factious combinations less to be dreaded in the former, than in the latter. The smaller the society, the fewer probably will be the distinct parties and interests composing it; the fewer the distinct parties and interests, the more frequently will a majority be found of the same party; and the smaller the number of individuals composing a majority, and the smaller the compass within which they are placed, the more easily will they concert and execute their plans of oppression. Extend the sphere, and you take in a greater variety of parties and interests; you make it less probable that a majority of the whole will have a common motive to invade the rights of other citizens; or if such a common motive exists, it will be more difficult for all who feel it to discover their own strength, and to act in unison with each other. Besides other impediments, it may be remarked,

---

[7] **aggregate**—collective; formed by the collection of different parts into a whole.

that where there is a consciousness of unjust or dishonourable purposes, communication is always checked by distrust, in proportion to the number whose concurrence is necessary.

Hence it clearly appears, that the same advantage, which a republic has over a democracy, in controlling the effects of faction, is enjoyed by a large over a small republic—is enjoyed by the union over the states composing it. Does this advantage consist in the substitution of representatives, whose enlightened views and virtuous sentiments render them superior to local prejudices, and to schemes of injustice? It will not be denied, that the representation of the union will be most likely to possess these requisite endowments. Does it consist in the greater security afforded by a greater variety of parties, against the event of any one party being able to outnumber and oppress the rest? In an equal degree does the encreased variety of parties, comprised within the union, encrease this security. Does it, in fine, consist in the greater obstacles opposed to the concert and accomplishment of the secret wishes of an unjust and interested majority? Here, again, the extent of the union gives it the most palpable advantage.

The influence of factious leaders may kindle a flame within their particular states, but will be unable to spread a general **conflagration**[8] through the other states: A religious sect, may degenerate into a political faction in a part of the confederacy; but the variety of sects dispersed over the entire face of it, must secure the national councils against any danger from that source: A rage for paper money, for an abolition of debts, for an equal division of property, or for any other improper or wicked project, will be less apt to pervade the whole body of the union, than a particular member of it; in the sample

---

[8] **conflagration**—large fire.

proportion as such a malady is more likely to taint a particular county or district, than an entire state.

In the extent and proper structure of the union, therefore, we behold a republican remedy for the diseases most incident to republican government. And according to the degree of pleasure and pride, we feel in being republicans, ought to be our zeal in cherishing the spirit, and supporting the character of federalists.

Publius.

QUESTIONS TO CONSIDER

1. What, according to Madison, are the main differences between a "pure democracy" and a republic?

2. How is representation handled in a republic?

3. How can a republican system of government help to overcome factions, local prejudices, and self-interest?

Antifederalist Viewpoint

BY RICHARD HENRY LEE

One of those who opposed the Constitution was the prominent Virginia legislator Richard Henry Lee. He had been very active throughout the revolutionary years of the new nation. As a delegate to the Continental Congresses, he had introduced the resolution to declare independence, the resolution to form foreign alliances for support during the war, and the resolution to prepare a plan of confederation. His was a powerful objecting voice. In a letter to Virginia Governor Edmund Randolph in October 1787, he gave his reasons.

New York, Oct. 16th, 1787
Dear Sir,

I was duly honoured with your favour of September 17th, from Philadelphia, which should have been acknowledged long before now, if the nature of the business it related to had not required time. The establishment of the new plan of government, in its present form, is a question that involves such immense consequences, to the present times and to posterity, that it calls for the deepest attention of the best and wisest friends of their country and mankind. If it be found right, after mature deliberation, adopt it; if wrong, amend it at all events: for to say that a bad government must be established for fear of **anarchy,**[1] is really saying that we should kill ourselves for fear of dying! Experience, and the actual state of things, show that there is no difficulty in procuring a general convention, the late one having been collected without any obstruction; nor does external war, or internal discord, prevent the most cool, collected, full, and fair discussion of this all-important subject. If, with infinite ease, a convention was obtained to prepare a system, why may not another convention, with equal ease, be obtained to make proper and necessary amendments? Good government is not the work of short time, or of sudden thought. From Moses to Montesquieu the greatest geniuses have been employed on this difficult subject, and yet experience has shown capital defects in the systems produced for the government of mankind. But since it is neither prudent nor easy to make frequent changes in government, and as bad governments have been generally found the most fixed, so it becomes of the last importance to frame the first establishment upon grounds the most unexceptionable, and such as the best theories with experience justify; not trusting, as our new constitution does, and as many approve of doing, to time and future events to correct errors that both reason and experience, in similar cases, now prove to exist in the new system. It has hitherto been supposed a fundamental truth that, in governments rightly balanced, the different branches of legislature should be unconnected, and that the legislative and executive powers should be separate. In the new constitution, the president and senate have all the executive and two-thirds of the legislative; and in

---

[1] **anarchy**—lawlessness or political disorder due to lack of governmental authority.

some weighty instances (as making all kinds of treaties which are to be the laws of the land) they have the whole legislative and executive powers. They jointly appoint all officers, civil and military, and they (the senate) try all **impeachments,**[2] either of their own members or of the officers appointed by themselves. Is there not a most formidable combination of power thus created in a few? and can the most critical eye, if a candid one, discover responsibility is this potent corps? or will any sensible man say that great power, without responsibility, can be given to rulers with safety to liberty? It is most clear that the parade of impeachment is nothing to them, or any of them, as little restraint is to be found, I presume, from the fear of offending **constituents.**[3]

The president is of four years duration, and Virginia (for example) has one vote, out of thirteen, in the choice of him. The senate is a body of six years duration, and as, in the choice of president, the largest state has but a thirteenth part, so is it in the choice of senators; and this thirteenth vote, not of the people, but of electors, two removes from the people. This latter statement is adduced to show that responsibility is as little to be apprehended from amenability to constituents, as from the terror of impeachment. You are, therefore, sir, well warranted in saying that either a monarchy or aristocracy will be generated: perhaps the most grievous system of government may arise! It cannot be denied, with truth, that this new constitution is, in its first principles, most highly and dangerously **oligarchic;**[4] and it is a point agreed that a government of the few is, of all governments, the worst. The only check to be found in

---

[2] **impeachments**—charges brought against public officials relating to misconduct in office.

[3] **constituents**—those who are represented by the elected officials.

[4] **oligarchic**—like a government in which a small group exercises control, especially for selfish or corrupt purposes.

favour of the democratic principle, in this system, is the House of Representatives, which, I believe, may justly be called a mere shred or rag of representation, it being obvious, to the least examination, that smallness of number, and great comparative disparity of power, renders that house of little effect to promote good, or restrain bad government. . . .

In this congressional legislature a bare majority can enact commercial laws, so that the representatives of the seven northern states, as they will have a majority, can, by law, create the most oppressive monopolies upon the five southern states, whose circumstances and productions are essentially different from theirs, although not a single man of their voters are the representatives of, or amenable to, the people of the southern states. Can such a set of men be, with the least colour of truth, called representatives of those they make laws for? It is supposed that the policy of the northern states will prevent such abuses! but how feeble, sir, is policy when opposed to interest among trading people, and what is the restraint arising from policy? It is said that we may be forced, by abuse, to become ship-builders; but how long will it be before a people of agriculture can produce ships sufficient to export such bulky and such extensive commodities as ours; and if we had the ships, from whence are the seamen to come? four thousand of whom, at least, we shall want in Virginia. In questions so liable to abuses, why was not the necessary vote put to two-thirds of the members of the legislature? Upon the while, sir, my opinion is, that, as this constitution abounds with useful regulations, at the same time that it is liable to strong and fundamental objections, the plan for us to pursue will be to propose the necessary amendments, and express our willingness to adopt it with the amendments; and to suggest the calling of a new convention for the purpose of considering them. To this I see no well-founded objection, but great safety and much good to be the probable result. I am perfectly satisfied that you make such use of this letter as you shall think to be for the public good. And now, after begging your pardon for so great a trespass on your patience, and presenting my best respects to your lady, I will conclude with assuring you that

I am, with the sincerest esteem and regard,

dear sir,
Your most affectionate and obediant servant.

QUESTIONS TO CONSIDER

1. What are Richard Henry Lee's objections to the new Constitution?

2. Lee feels the proposed Constitution neither balances power between the different legislative branches nor provides for separation of power between the legislative and the executive branches. Explain whether you agree and why.

3. Lee argues that the length of government officials' terms of office could lead to too much power in the hands of a small group of individuals, as in an oligarchy or a monarchy. Do you think this has happened in our government? Explain.

4. How does Lee represent his region of the country in his arguments of the last paragraph of this letter?

Virginia's Recommendations for a Bill of Rights

BY REPRESENTATIVES OF THE PEOPLE OF VIRGINIA

The Constitution did not include a bill of rights. The Federalists thought it was not necessary because the state constitutions all had one. The Antifederalists, fearing a strong central government, believed a bill of rights was essential. Representatives of the people of Virginia made a formal proposal, included here. It suggested 20 rights. Many states ratified the Constitution only after the Federalists promised to add such a bill. When Madison later sat down to draft the Bill of Rights, he studied as many as 80 different items from the various state constitutions.

Virginia's Recommendations for a Bill of Rights (1788)

We the Delegates of the People of Virginia duly elected in pursuance of a recommendation from the General Assembly and now met in Convention having fully and freely investigated and discussed the proceedings of the Federal Convention and being prepared as well as the most mature deliberation hath enabled us to decide thereon do in the name and in behalf of the People of Virginia declare and make known that the powers granted under the Constitution being derived from the People of the United States may be resumed by them whensoever the same shall be perverted to their injury or oppression and that every power not granted thereby remains with them and at their will: that therefore no right of any denomination can be cancelled abridged restrained or modified by the Congress by the Senate or House of Representatives acting in any Capacity by the President or any Department or Officer of the United States except in those instances in which power is given by the Constitution for those purposes: & that among other essential rights the liberty of Conscience and of the Press cannot be cancelled abridged restrained or modified by any authority of the United States. With these impressions with a solemn appeal to the Searcher of hearts for the purity of our intentions and under the conviction that whatsoever imperfections may exist in the Constitution ought rather to be examined in the mode prescribed therein than to bring the Union into danger by a delay with a hope of obtaining Amendments previous to the Ratification, We the said Delegates in the name and in behalf of the People of Virginia do by these presents assent to and ratify the Constitution recommended on the seventeenth day of September one thousand seven hundred and eighty seven by the Federal Convention for the Government of the United States. . . .

Subsequent Amendments agreed to in Convention as necessary to the proposed Constitution of Government for the United States, recommended to the consideration of the Congress which shall first assemble under the said Constitution to be acted upon according to the mode prescribed in the fifth article thereof:

Videlicet [that is to say];

That there be a Declaration or Bill of Rights asserting and securing from encroachment the essential and unalienable Rights of the People in some such manner as the following;

First, That there are certain natural rights of which men, when they form a social compact cannot deprive or divest their posterity, among which are the enjoyment of life and liberty; with the means of acquiring, possessing and protecting property, and pursuing and obtaining happiness and safety.

Second, That all power is naturally vested in and consequently derived from the people; that Magistrates, therefore, are their trustees and agents and at all times amenable to them.

Third, That Government ought to be instituted for the common benefit, protection and security of the People; and that the doctrine of non-resistance against arbitrary power and oppression is absurd slavish, and destructive of the good and happiness of mankind.

Fourth, That no man or set of Men are entitled to exclusive or separate public **emoluments**[1] or privileges from the community, but in Consideration of public services; which not being descendible, neither ought the offices of Magistrate, Legislator or Judge, or any other public office to be hereditary.

Fifth, That the legislative, executive, and judiciary powers of Government should be separate and distinct, and that the members of the two first may be restrained from oppression by feeling and participating the public burthens, they should, at fixt periods be reduced to a private station, return into the mass of

---

[1] **emoluments**—advantages; perks.

the people; and the vacancies be supplied by certain and regular elections; in which all or any part of the former members to be eligible or ineligible, as the rules of the Constitution of Government, and the laws shall direct.

Sixth, That elections of representatives in the legislature ought to be free and frequent, and all men having sufficient evidence of permanent common interest with and attachment to the Community ought to have the right of **suffrage:**[2] and no aid, charge, tax or fee can be set, rated, or levied upon the people without their own consent, or that of their representatives so elected, nor can they be bound by any law to which they have not in like manner assented for the public good.

Seventh, That all power of suspending laws or the execution of laws by any authority without the consent of the representatives of the people in the legislature is injurious to their rights, and ought not to be exercised.

Eighth, That in all capital and criminal prosecutions, a man hath a right to demand the cause and nature of his accusation, to be confronted with the accusers and witnesses, to call for evidence and be allowed counsel in his favor, and to a fair and speedy trial by an impartial Jury of his vicinage,[3] without whose unanimous consent he cannot be found guilty, (except in the government of the land and naval forces) nor can he be compelled to give evidence against himself.

Ninth, That no freeman ought to be taken, imprisoned, or disseised [dispossessed] of his freehold, liberties, privileges or franchises, or outlawed or exiled, or in any manner destroyed or deprived of his life, liberty or property but by the law of the land.

Tenth, That every freeman restrained of his liberty is entitled, to a remedy to enquire into the lawfulness

---

[2] **suffrage**—voting.

[3] vicinage—vicinity.

thereof, and to remove the same, if unlawful, and that such remedy ought not to be denied nor delayed.

Eleventh, That in controversies respecting property and in suits between man and man, the ancient trial by Jury is one of the greatest Securities to the rights of the people, and ought to remain sacred and inviolable.

Twelfth, That every freeman ought to find a certain remedy by recourse to the laws for all injuries and wrongs he may receive in his person, property or character. He ought to obtain right and justice freely without sale, compleatly and without denial, promptly and without delay, and that all establishments or regulations **contravening**[4] these rights, are oppressive and unjust.

Thirteenth, That excessive Bail ought not be required, nor excessive fines imposed, nor cruel and unusual punishments inflicted.

Fourteenth, That every freeman has a right to be secure from all unreasonable searches and seizures of his person, his papers and his property; all warrants, therefore, to search suspected places, or seize any freeman, his papers or property without information upon Oath (or affirmation of a person religiously scrupulous of taking an oath) of legal and sufficient cause, are grievous and oppressive; and all general Warrants to search suspected places, or to apprehend any suspected person, without specially naming or describing the place or person, are dangerous and ought not to be granted.

Fifteenth, That the people have a right peaceably to assemble together to consult for the common good, or to instruct their Representatives, and that every freeman has a right to petition or apply to the legislature for redress of grievances.

Sixteenth, That the people have a right to freedom of speech, and of writing and publishing their Sentiments;

---

[4] **contravening**—violating; in opposition to.

but the freedom of the press is one of the greatest **bulwarks**[5] of liberty and ought not to be violated.

Seventeenth, That the people have a right to keep and bear arms; that a well regulated Militia composed of the body of the people trained to arms is the proper, natural and safe defence of a free State. That standing armies in time of peace are dangerous to liberty, and therefore ought to be avoided, as far as the circumstances and protection of the Community will admit; and that in all cases the military should be under strict subordination to and governed by the Civil power.

Eighteenth, That no Soldier in time of peace ought to be quartered in any house without the consent of the owner, and in time of war in such manner only as the laws direct.

Nineteenth, That any person religiously scrupulous of bearing arms ought to be exempted upon payment of an equivalent to employ another to bear arms in his stead.

Twentieth, That religion or the duty which we owe to our Creator, and the manner of discharging it can be directed only by reason and conviction, not by force or violence, and therefore all men have an equal, natural and unalienable right to the free exercise of religion according to the dictates of conscience, and that no particular religious sect or society ought to be favored or established by Law in preference to others.

---

[5] **bulwarks**—supports or protections.

QUESTIONS TO CONSIDER

1. Why do the Antifederalists want a bill of rights?

2. Which of Virginia's twenty proposed items concern individual rights?

3. Which of these twenty proposed items do you think eventually made it into the Constitution?

What Is an American?

BY J. HECTOR ST. JOHN DE CRÈVECOEUR

De Crèvecoeur was a French officer and mapmaker in Canada
who chose to stay permanently in North America in 1759. As time
passed, he became a citizen of New York, married, and settled
down to farming and raising a family. When the Revolution came,
it tore his family apart. His wife and her relations were Loyalists.
Many of his friends were Patriots. In 1780 he left for Europe with
his son. There he wrote and published the essays that made him
famous. A work entitled Letters from an American Farmer
brought him to the attention of powerful people such as Benjamin
Franklin. He gained appointment as French consul to three of the
states in the new nation. In the following excerpt from one of
the most famous of his essays, he displays his enthusiasm, optimism,
and acceptance of new-world democracy. His words had a major
influence on how Americans saw themselves thereafter.

I wish I could be acquainted with the feelings and thoughts which must agitate the heart and present themselves to the mind of an enlightened Englishman, when he first lands on this continent. . . . He is arrived on a new continent; a modern society offers itself to his contemplation, different from what he had hitherto seen. It is not composed, as in Europe, of great lords who possess everything, and of a herd of people who have nothing. Here are no aristocratical families, no courts, no kings, no bishops, no **ecclesiastical**[1] dominion, no invisible power giving to a few a very visible one; no great manufacturers employing thousands, no great refinements of luxury. The rich and the poor are not so far removed from each other as they are in Europe. Some few towns excepted, we are all tillers of the earth, from Nova Scotia to West Florida. We are a people of cultivators, scattered over an immense territory, communicating with each other by means of good roads and navigable rivers, united by the silken bands of mild government, all respecting the laws, without dreading their power, because they are equitable. We are all animated with the spirit of an industry which is unfettered and unrestrained, because each person works for himself. If he travels through our rural districts he views not the hostile castle, and the haughty mansion, contrasted with the clay-built hut and miserable cabin, where cattle and men help to keep each other warm, and dwell in meanness, smoke, and **indigence.**[2] A pleasing uniformity of decent competence appears throughout our habitations. The meanest of our log-houses is a dry and comfortable habitation. Lawyer or merchant are the fairest titles our towns afford; that of a farmer is the only **appellation**[3] of the rural inhabitants of our country.

---

[1] **ecclesiastical**—churchly or religious.

[2] **indigence**—poverty.

[3] **appellation**—name or title.

It must take some time ere he can reconcile himself to our dictionary, which is but short in words of dignity, and names of honour. There, on a Sunday, he sees a congregation of respectable farmers and their wives, all clad in neat homespun, well mounted, or riding in their own humble waggons. There is not among them an esquire, saving the unlettered magistrate. There he sees a parson as simple as his flock, a farmer who does not riot on the labour of others. We have no princes, for whom we toil, starve, and bleed: we are the most perfect society now existing in the world . . .

. . . The Americans were once scattered all over Europe; here they are incorporated into one of the finest systems of population which has ever appeared, and which will hereafter become distinct by the power of the different climates they inhabit. The American ought therefore to love this country much better than that wherein either he or his forefathers were born. Here the rewards of his industry follow with equal steps the progress of his labour; his labour is founded on the basis of nature, self-interest; can it want a stronger allurement? Wives and children, who before in vain demanded of him a morsel of bread, now, fat and frolicsome, gladly help their father to clear those fields whence exuberant crops are to arise to feed and to clothe them all; without any part being claimed, either by a despotic prince, a rich abbot, or a mighty lord. Here religion demands but little of him; a small voluntary salary to the minister, and gratitude to God; can he refuse these? The American is a new man, who acts upon new principles; he must therefore entertain new ideas, and form new opinions. From involuntary idleness, servile dependence, **penury,**[4] and useless labour, he has passed to toils of a very different nature, rewarded by ample subsistence.—This is an American. . . .

---

[4] **penury**—severe poverty.

QUESTIONS TO CONSIDER

1. How does de Crèvecoeur support his claim that America is "the most perfect society now existing in the world"?

2. Does de Crèvecoeur's definition of what it means to be an American still apply today?

3. What positive qualities of American life would de Crèvecoeur add if he were writing today?

12 Adapted from *The Head and Heart of Thomas Jefferson* by John Dos Passos. Copyright 1954 by John Dos Passos. Used by permission of Doubleday, a division of Random House, Inc.

25 "Boston Has a Tea Party" from *Turning the World Upside Down* by John Tebbel. Copyright © 1993 by John Tebbel. Reprinted by permission of Crown Publishers, Inc.

65 "A Scattering of Sparks" from *Voices of 1776* by Richard Wheeler. (New York: Thomas Y. Crowell Co., 1972).

78 "Thomas Paine" from *Faces of Revolution* by Bernard Bailyn. Copyright © 1990 by Bernard Bailyn. Reprinted by permission of Alfred A. Knopf, Inc.

120 "The British Lamentation" from *The Isaiah Thomas Collection of Ballads* by Worthington C. Ford. Reprinted courtesy of American Antiquarian Society.

122 "Paul Jones's Victory" from *The Isaiah Thomas Collection of Ballads* by Worthington C. Ford. Reprinted courtesy of American Antiquarian Society.

133 "Times That Try Men's Souls" from *Turning the World Upside Down* by John Tebbel. Copyright © 1993 by John Tebbel. Reprinted by permission of Crown Publishers, Inc.

176 "The Delegates: A Kind of Brotherhood." Reprinted with the permission of Simon & Schuster, Inc. from *The Founding* by Fred Barbash. Copyright © 1987 by Fred Barbash.

191 "National Sins." Reprinted with the permission of Simon & Schuster, Inc. from *The Founding* by Fred Barbash. Copyright © 1987 by Fred Barbash.

Photo Research Diane Hamilton

Photos Courtesy of the Library of Congress.

Every effort has been made to secure complete rights and permissions for each selection presented herein. Updated acknowledgements, if needed, will appear in subsequent printings.

Index